P9-DHB-101

Also Available from EYE ON EDUCATION

What Great Principals Do *Differently*:
15 Things That Matter Most
Todd Whitaker

The Principal as Instructional Leader:
A Handbook for Supervisors, Second Edition
Sally J. Zepeda

What Successful Principals Do!
169 Tips for Principals
Franzy Fleck

Lead With Me:
A Principal's Guide to Teacher Leadership
Gayle Moller and Anita Pankake

The Instructional Leader's Guide
to Informal Classroom Observations
Sally J. Zepeda

Lead Me – I Dare You!
Sherrel Bergman and Judith Brough

From At-Risk to Academic Excellence:
What Successful Leaders Do
Schargel, Thacker, and Bell

Improving Your School One Week at a Time:
Building the Foundation for Professional Teaching & Learning
Jeffrey Zoul

Cornerstones of Strong Schools:
Practices for Purposeful Leadership
Jeffrey Zoul and Laura Link

Countdown to the Principalship:
A Resource Guide for Beginning Principals
O'Rourke, Provenzano, Bellamy, and Ballek

The Principal's Purpose:
A Practical Guide to Moral and Ethical Leadership
Leanna Stohr Isaacson

Smart, Fast, Efficient:
The New Principals' Guide to Success
Leanna Stohr Isaacson

Creating the High Schools of Our Choice
Tim Westerberg

BRAVO Principal!
Sandra Harris

The Administrator's Guide
to School Community Relations, Second Edition
George E. Pawlas

School Leader Internship: Developing, Monitoring,
and Evaluating Your Leadership Experience, Second Ed.
Martin, Wright, Danzig, Flanary, and Brown

Talk It Out!
The Educator's Guide to Successful Difficult Conversations
Barbara E. Sanderson

Making the Right Decisions:
A Guide for School Leaders
Douglas J. Fiore and Chip Joseph

Dealing with Difficult Teachers, Second Edition
Todd Whitaker

Dealing with Difficult Parents
(And With Parents in Difficult Situations)
Todd Whitaker and Douglas Fiore

Great Quotes for Great Educators
Todd Whitaker and Dale Lumpa

Elevating Student Voice:
How to Enhance Participation, Citizenship, & Leadership
Nelson Beaudoin

Stepping Outside Your Comfort Zone:
Lessons for School Leaders
Nelson Beaudoin

What Great Teachers Do *Differently*:
14 Things That Matter Most
Todd Whitaker

Data Analysis for Continuous School Improvement
Victoria L. Bernhardt

About the Author

Frank Buck has served as a central office administrator, principal, assistant principal, and band director during a career in education spanning more than 25 years. He has served as an Editorial Advisor for the National Association of Elementary School Principals. His nationally-published articles are aimed at helping school leaders become better organized and better managers of their time. The workshops Dr. Buck has conducted over the past decade have drawn rave reviews from teachers and school administrators for their practicality and the simplicity of the message he conveys.

Dr. Buck resides in Pell City, Alabama and serves as a central office administrator for the Talladega City School System. He may be contacted for workshops or speaking engagements through his blog: http://FrankBuck. blogspot.com

Dedication

This book is dedicated to my wife and best friend, Davonia. Her love and encouragement over the last 19 years have been a constant source of joy and inspiration.

Table of Contents

Preface

Good-bye, Sir, excuse me, I haven't time.
I'll come back, I can't wait, I haven't time.
I must end this letter—I haven't time.
I'd love to help you, but I haven't time.
I can't accept, having no time.
I can't think, I can't read, I'm swamped, I haven't time.
I'd like to pray, but I haven't time.

Michel Quoist

In *The Harried Leisure Class*, Staffan Linder begins with the preceding poem. The time constraints, and feelings that accompany them, are typical of our culture. In the nearly 40 years that have passed since that book's publication, the frantic pace of society has only grown worse. Each passing year seems to bring more demands on our time. Technology, with its promise of making our lives easier, has provided us with cell phones that ring constantly, a daily barrage of e-mails, and a general overload of information.

It is possible not only to survive but to thrive in an age of limited time and unlimited demands. This book shows how with specific tools aimed at organizing surroundings and managing time. In the process, the overwhelmed school leader may well find relief from much of the stress caused by the *time crunch*.

Many published books address personal organization and time management. These topics are also favorite subjects of magazine articles. Such popularity illustrates both the importance of these topics to our culture as well as how elusive mastering them can be.

My purpose in writing this book is to fill a void in the literature. Too often, time-management books target the business executive. Although it is true that those in the educational arena share many of the same challenges, it is also true that schools are unique places. This book is written for *school leaders*. Its scenarios specifically address the day-to-day situations school leaders face on a regular basis.

Time-management books tend to offer a smorgasbord of suggestions, yet fail to provide the necessary depth to make a difference for the reader. This book provides the school leader with a complete system for managing time, getting organized, and staying organized.

Finally, the role of technology in our lives has increased exponentially in a relatively few years. The hallmark books on time management and organization from decades past are unable to help us in this area. Publications such as this one are needed to address both the problems technology poses and the opportunities to harness the capabilities technology can offer.

This book does not eliminate the time demands that go hand in hand with this profession. What it can do is provide some tools and techniques to help the busy school leader more efficiently and effectively address those demands. The results are a feeling of being in control of the day, a decrease in stress, and an increase in the sheer joy that school leadership can offer. Moreover, the school leader can find more time to spend on that which is truly significant—perhaps on some of the options outlined in the poem that began this section.

1

Time Management and Organization: Challenges for School Leaders

Who Is a School Leader?

The title for this book was chosen deliberately. This book is for *school leaders*. What exactly does the term mean? A *school leader* can be found holding a number of positions. Obviously, the school superintendent is in this category. Also, principals, assistant principals, and central office administrators are likely candidates. A school leader is also a department head who is balancing the roles of teaching with those of shaping the direction of a curricular area. A school leader is also a classroom teacher who assumes responsibility for sponsoring a club or activity that benefits the student body. Likewise, the person who is developing ideas and sharing them with colleagues wears the mantle of leadership.

In short, a *school leader* is someone who steps forward to help shape the direction of what happens in schools, regardless of the title on the job description. Once that first step is taken, the opportunities multiply. As the opportunities multiply, the tasks increase in number and complexity. Without intervention, the complexity can become overwhelming. The school leader needs the tools to simplify the complex.

The Universal Time Crunch

If you feel the crunch of too much to do and too little time in which to do it, welcome to a large club. In the 1972 classic *The Time Trap*, Alec Mackenzie states, "Of the thousands of managers I have polled, from board chairmen and chief executives to first-line supervisors, only one in a hundred has enough time." Peter Drucker's 1966 hallmark work *The Effective Executive* tells us that "effective executives . . . do not start with their tasks. They start with their time." Drucker goes on to say, "Nothing else, perhaps, distinguishes effective executives as much as their tender loving care of time." What Mackenzie and Drucker found to be true in the business world then is just as true in the arena of education today.

Organization, Time Management, and the Art of Leadership

School leadership has been the topic of books too numerous to count. The subject has been approached from such varied standpoints as curriculum development, effective hiring, professional development of teachers, improving school climate, understanding the nature of student learning, involving parents in meaningful ways, and understanding the laws that affect us. Furthermore, what was true in any of these areas at one point in time may be quite different a decade later. Few things are constant in education. There is one element, however, that is unchanging. That element is time.

Some may dismiss attention to organization and time management as being separate from leadership and the achievement of a vision for the school or school system. Nothing could be farther from the truth. For the school leader, every good thing we do for our students, our school systems, our communities, our families, and ourselves is accomplished through the dimension of time. Furthermore, time is finite. We cannot buy, beg, borrow, or steal anymore. We can only manage the 168 hours we are given each week. Our ability to plan, enlist the help of others, and achieve a vision is directly related to our ability to efficiently organize our environments and effectively use time.

How This Book Can Help

The ability to organize and manage time is crucial to our professional success. Unfortunately, these critical skills are typically not taught in colleges or education. For the past decade, I have led workshops in these areas. The feedback I have received from participants is that the tools shared with them truly do make a difference in their productivity.

In this book, I share those tools with you. After reading the book, you will have a comprehensive system for bringing order and control to your personal and professional life. What you read in this book is practical and easy to implement. Finally, you can immediately put this material into practice.

2

Clear Your Desk

Executives waste six weeks per year searching for lost documents.

Fast Company, August 2004

For those looking for ways to save time, organizing the work area is a great start. The quote that begins this chapter illustrates the problem caused when paperwork is out of control. How great it would be if the papers that sit on our desks would go away and magically come back exactly when we need them! That is exactly what this first tool does.

I first saw this concept as a young boy hanging out at my dad's office. He was a lawyer operating in a one-man shop. He had no secretary and handled every aspect of his practice by himself. I noticed that first thing each morning he opened one filing cabinet drawer. In that drawer were files labeled with numbers from 1 through 31. If the date was the 15th day of the month, he pulled out the 15 folder. In that folder were papers related to the various people he would be seeing that day. Every piece of paper he would be working with that day was contained in that folder.

I thought my dad originated this idea, and it was one I put into practice from my first day as a teacher and have never left it. Later, I learned that it is an old and very common tool in the business world called the *tickler file.*

Setting Up a Tickler File

Creating a tickler file requires 43 folders. The first 31 are to be labeled 1 to 31, with each file representing a day of the month. The remaining 12 folders represent the 12 months of the year and are labeled January through December. The system is ready to go.

When paper arrives that will be needed sometimes in the future, decide when you would like to see the paper again and drop it into the appropriate file. If that day is going to be within the next month, slip the paper into the correct numbered folder. A piece of paper dropped into folder 17 resurfaces on the 17th day of the month. For papers needed again in a month or more, slip the paper into the correct monthly folder. The paper that you do not need to see again until sometime in November is filed in the November folder.

At the end of the month, empty the folder for the next month into the 1 to 31 folders. For example, at the end of February, open the March file, make a decision about what day in March you need to see each item, and file each one in the 1 to 31 folders.

Tickler files must be kept close at hand so that papers can be dropped into them throughout the day. For this reason, I keep mine in a hanging file drawer right in the desk. Hanging files offer several advantages. The user does not have to worry about their standing upright. Their sturdy construction makes them excellent for steady use. Finally, the user may place inside the hanging file manila file folders containing papers related to a particular project.

Tickler Files in Action

Let's begin with an example that is all too common. Imagine receiving the memo outlined in Figure 2.1.

Figure 2.1. Memo to Principals

Memo

To: Principals

From: Superintendent

Please complete this form and bring it with you to the administrative meeting on Tuesday.

This job actually has two parts:

1. Complete the form.
2. Bring the form to the meeting.

Completing the form is something that could probably be done on the spot. In fact, if a task will take only a few minutes to complete, complete it when it first appears. If you are going to take the time to look at it, completing it right then saves refamiliarizing yourself with it later.

The second part of the task is the part that causes the trouble. The form has been completed and today is only Wednesday. What are you going to do with this piece of paper from now until Tuesday of next week?

In all too many offices and classrooms, the drill resembles the following scenario. The paper is carefully placed on the corner of the desk so as not to be forgotten. For the next half day, that paper is moved around in an effort to find other papers under and around it. You look up from the current work countless times and see that piece of paper, each time thinking about how you must remember to take it to the meeting next week. Just after lunch, something gets placed on top of it. You have just experienced the beginning of the end!

By Monday, this piece of paper is buried seven layers down and has not been given a thought in days. You leave for your meeting, and guess what is still buried on your desk? You realize dropping papers on the corner of the desk doesn't work!

The next time, you try a different approach. "I'll tape it to the wall," you think. "That way it won't get lost." This time, as you leave for your meeting, and where is the form? In all too many cases, it is still taped to the wall. One rule of thumb in organizing is that whatever is taped to a wall becomes part of the décor!

An easier way exists. In this case, we need this paper to resurface on Tuesday. Simply drop it in the tickler file which corresponds to Tuesday's date. It is out of sight and out of mind. Furthermore, it is not cluttering the desk or decorating the wall. On Tuesday morning, you pull the folder for that day, dump it on your desk, and there is the form along with the other papers needed for that day.

Other Examples

What else might be placed in the tickler files? Here is a partial list of possibilities:

- ◆ You receive tickets to an event that occurs 3 weeks from now. Drop them in the numbered file corresponding to the date of the event.

On that date, the tickets appear. You don't have to carry them in your wallet for fear of losing (or forgetting) them. On the day they are needed, they appear.

♦ You can buy birthday cards for all of your friends and relatives with one trip to the card shop. After arriving at home, address all the envelopes and attach return address labels to the whole batch. Pencil in the date each card must go in the mail in the spot where the postage stamp will later go. Simply drop the cards in the appropriate tickler folders. Throughout the year, cards keep popping up on the exact days they need to go in the mail. You will never forget a birthday again!

♦ You are attending a workshop and have a flyer outlining the driving directions. You will need that item on the day of the workshop, so put it in the tickler file. It appears the morning of the workshop.

♦ You are completing a report and do not have all the information needed. Jot down in your planner what information you need to obtain and make a plan for how to get it. Slip the report into a tickler file. When the report resurfaces, you have the information and can complete the report.

♦ You have prepared a *problem of the day* for your classes. Drop each one in the appropriate tickler file.

♦ You have prepared a test and need to duplicate it, but the copier will be out of order until Thursday. Drop the test in the file for Thursday. It is out of sight and out of mind until the day you can do something about it.

♦ You duplicate the test on Thursday even though you won't be giving the test until Wednesday of next week (After all, that copier could go down again!). Put the tests in a manila folder and put the whole folder in next Wednesday's tickler.

Morning Ritual

Let us say that you arrive at work on the morning of September 27th. Figure 2.2 illustrates how your tickler files will look.

Figure 2.2. Example of Tickler File

Because today is September 27th, the 27 folder is in the front of the drawer. Place it on the desk and take out the papers. The 27 folder now goes in the back, right behind folder 26. It now represents October 27th.

You have on your desk all the papers that you decided you should see on September 27th. There on the desk, you find the following:

- ◆ The card that needs to go in the mail today.
- ◆ The tickets to tonight's concert.
- ◆ The driving directions for how to get to the concert.
- ◆ The folder of materials to discuss with Penelope's mom, with whom you have a conference this afternoon.
- ◆ The phone message to call Mr. Jones. When you tried to call him last week, his secretary said he would be out of town until the 27th.

You may prefer to check the tickler file at the end of the workday. In that case, just before going home on the 26th, pull the folder for the 27th and handle its contents. Just before leaving for the day, leave the item you want to work on the first thing the following morning squarely in the middle of the desk.

Forgetting Is a Good Thing

Much of the stress we feel is related to the many responsibilities we are expected to remember. From the examples you have seen, tickler files relieve that stress by doing the remembering for you. When you drop a piece of paper in the tickler file, you can now forget about it. In fact, the entire system outlined in this book requires you to remember exactly two things. One of them is to check the tickler file first thing in the morning. The second is to look at the signature tool, either paper or digital, examined in the upcoming two chapters.

Three Little Boxes

Tickler files allow for a clean desktop. During the day, however, you deal with three types of paperwork that need storage places:

1. New paperwork coming your way
2. Papers from today's tickler file that cannot be completed immediately
3. Work you produce that needs to go to someone else

Three boxes organize the three types of paperwork:

In

In provides a place to throw anything new. The benefit is that you can continue to focus on the task at hand without being distracted by every piece of paper that comes your way. During the typical day, the school leader has a variety of items cross the desk:

♦ Today's mail

♦ Memos from others in the organization

♦ Notes from parents

♦ Phone messages

If you stop to examine and handle every piece of paper as it arrives, the constant interruptions prevent you from accomplishing much of anything. *In* provides a spot where all the incoming barrage can be housed until you are ready to deal with it.

In can take a number of physical forms. An inexpensive letter tray is an excellent choice. A file folder works. An empty desk drawer is also a possibility. Building-level administrators may place *In* near the administrative assistant. Others can drop notes or other papers in there without interrupting the administrator.

Getting to the bottom of the Inbox must be *one single activity*. It should be completed within *less than half an hour*. Many people complain of never being able to reach the bottom of the Inbox. The great fear is that somewhere toward the bottom lurks an emergency. The secret here is to make a decision on what each piece of paper represents:

- Junk mail goes immediately into the trash can. Throw away virtually all catalogs. Use the Internet to search vendors' sites there rather than filing catalogs and purging them when new ones arrive.

- Items that can be handled by other people are tagged with an appropriate note to them and placed in *Out*.

- Quick phone messages may be handled as soon as you touch the piece of paper. Depending on the nature of call, you can often continue handling other papers while carrying on the conversation.

- Reading material should be placed together. Before leaving for a meeting, grab some reading material. While waiting for a meeting to start, waiting at a doctor's office, or waiting for a train to pass, having reading material at hand turns wasted time into productive time.

- Items to be handled on some future day are placed in the appropriate tickler file.

- Some items take more time to complete. Make a quick decision on what needs to be done, add the item to the task list, and then place the paper into *Pending*.

Pending

Some papers cannot be acted on immediately yet might be needed later in the day. *Pending* provides a holding tank for them. For example, today's tickler file includes papers related to a conference to be held with Penelope's mother this afternoon. *Pending* provides a place to put those papers until the time of the conference. *Pending* could be a letter tray. A desk drawer can just as easily be devoted to this function.

Out

This box houses the papers that need to go somewhere else other than the office (or classroom). These items could include the following:

- Outgoing mail
- Material for someone else to file
- Papers for somewhere in the building
- Items to take home

At one or more times during the day, emptying *Out* should be one single activity. As with *In* and *Pending, Out* can be a letter tray, desk drawer, folder, or neat stack placed under a decorative paperweight on a nearby table.

After having conducted countless workshops, participants tell me that instituting tickler files has made a significant difference in their ability to organize the paper in their lives. As a fellow practitioner, this tool has allowed me to work with a clean desktop and a clear head my entire career.

Chapter 6 examines a second function for tickler files. This second function also calls for a second label for the files. This point is clarified in that chapter.

Next Steps

- Answer this question for yourself: "What on your desk at this moment should go in a tickler file?"
- Select a place to house your tickler files. Do you have a file drawer in your desk? If not, do you have a filing cabinet you can access while still sitting at your desk?
- Secure 43 folders, preferably hanging files. Do not label them yet. Chapter 6 examines a second function for your tickler files and a second label for each.
- Establish *In*, *Out*, and *Pending* boxes.

3

Your Signature Tool: Organizing With Paper

The master thinker knows that ideas are elusive and often
quickly forgotten, so he traps them with notebook and
pencil. He heeds the Chinese proverb: "The strongest mind
is weaker than the palest ink."

Wilferd A. Peterson, Adventures in the Art of Living

The single biggest personal productivity suggestion I can offer is to acquire the habit of immediately writing things down. Be it an idea, a phone number, a task to be done, or a date to be saved, as soon as the brain thinks it, we must instinctively write it down. Any organizational system is going to have this premise at its root.

From there, the trick simply becomes how to organize what has been written so we see what we need to see when we need to see it. If mastered, others see us as being in control, relaxed, and on top of our game. If we are slack in this area, we find ourselves constantly searching for information. Our notes are scattered across random memos pads, sticky notes, and backs of discarded envelopes. We are frustrated, seen by others as not quite having it all together, and wind up spending far too much time and showing far too little gain in any area of our responsibilities.

This chapter is about designing and using a *signature tool*. It serves as the one place to trap any new appointment, task, or piece of information. This tool turns forgetting from being a bad thing to a well-deserved right. Once your signature tool traps the item, your brain can forget about it and move on to more productive, creative thinking. The term *signature tool* is used for an important reason. If used to its full potential, it will be with you wherever you are. Others notice that it appears from your pocket or purse anytime you need to jot down a new commitment or check an existing one. Those who know you well will realize that when they see that tool appear, the new commitment about which the two of you are talking will not *slip through the cracks.*

A signature tool can take a number of forms. Chapter 4 examines digital options, such as a Palm or BlackBerry. This chapter is devoted to paper options. Whatever form one's signature tool takes, it is indispensable in a world where our commitments are great, our time is precious, and the consequences for *dropping the ball* can be costly. Our signature tool prevents us from awakening at 3:00 AM worried about what we have forgotten to do. It allows us to focus on the task at hand, fully confident that everything else will *keep.*

Paper or Digital?

We live in a world that is becoming increasingly more digital. At the same time, paper continues to be a trusted medium. Should your system be paper based or electronic? Valid arguments exist for each camp. Paper requires no special tools or any software to learn. Input is effortless. A paper system is inexpensive. Finally, many people simply like the feel of paper.

Those who digitally organize argue they never have to recopy data. They can import any digital data into the system. They can share their data by pasting it into a simple e-mail. They have a calendar that extends far into the future. A handheld device is light and portable while still holding a tremendous amount of data. The search capabilities are extraordinary. Finally, they can easily back up their data.

Five Functions and Five Guiding Principles

Regardless of whether a paper or electronic tool is used, a signature tool must be able to perform five functions:

1. *Remind us of appointments.* Every calendar is capable of this function.
2. *Display our tasks (or to-do items).* In this area most monthly calendars are inadequate. The volume of tasks the school leader is expected to handle is simply too large to be housed on a monthly or even

week-at-a-glance calendar. Day-at-a-glance calendars offer an advantage in this area.

3. *Remind us of tasks delegated to others.* As school leaders we cannot do everything ourselves. We enlist the help of others to accomplish goals. How can we keep up with the responsibilities of each person? After ordering materials from a vendor, how can we keep track of what has been ordered, what has been received, and if the billing is correct? Others borrow books and other resources from us. How can we remember what we have loaned, to whom it has been loaned, and what has been returned? Most importantly, how can we make all these challenges easy?

4. *Allow us to record and retrieve communication.* As school leaders, we are involved in conferences with parents and teachers. We attend meetings and speak about important matters on the telephone. Since our first days in the classroom, we have been told to document. Unfortunately, few of us have been shown any system that allows us to document quickly and easily and then later retrieve what we have recorded.

5. *Help us manage goals.* School leaders set goals as a matter of course. Accomplishing any one of them involves a number of steps and managing a certain amount of accompanying information. The challenge becomes even greater in that we are usually pursuing multiple goals and engaged in multiple projects at any one time.

Regardless of the tool, five guiding principles are essential for any organizational system:

1. *Use only one system.* All calendar events, whether personal or professional should be placed on the same calendar. The same principle holds true of to-do items. As soon two calendars are used, it is nearly impossible to be sure whether the one in hand is complete. In short, the person who uses two calendars cannot trust either one.

2. *The system must be portable.* It goes from school to home and back. It goes to faculty meetings and to the grocery store. If it is bulky, you will likely leave it on your desk.

3. *Keep the system handy.* The system is of little good if it is not with you.

4. *Get rid of scraps of paper.* Write it all in your system. We are tempted to grab the first Post-it Note or back of an envelope to jot the thing we must remember. Within 15 minutes we cannot find the scrap of paper. Everything must go in the system.

5. *Let the system do the remembering.* We cause ourselves unneeded stress by trying to keep track of our varied responsibilities in our heads.

When an obligation first comes to our attention, we must enter it in the system right then. It is a habit that must be developed. The reward is that when we enter something into our system, we can forget about it.

This chapter concentrates on three functions of the signature tool: (1) the calendar, (2) the task list, and (3) daily documentation.

Choosing a Signature Tool

My personal choice for a paper-based tool is the Day-Timer organizer. The left-hand page provides ample space for calendar items and lines to record tasks. The right-hand page is for documentation. The loose-leaf format allows extra pages to be inserted.

The Calendar

When talking about keeping a calendar, clarity is king. We must be able to look at the page and see at a glance what blocks of time are *set in stone*. A common mistake is to litter the calendar page with a variety of to-do items and random notes. To achieve clarity, limit the calendar to three types of items:

1. *Appointments*: When we are expected to be at a certain place at a certain time, that obligation goes in the calendar. We are accustomed to these kinds of things. The conference with John's mother Tuesday at 3:00 and the dental appointment October 12 at 4:00 are examples.

2. *Tasks that absolutely must be done that day*: When the postmark deadline for the grant proposal is 5:00 PM today and the finishing touches have yet to be put on the document, we block out a time on the calendar. With a glance at the calendar, we can see that block of time is committed and will not schedule another activity for the same block of time.

3. *Things that need to be known about the day*: Mrs. Jones is having a guest speaker in her class. Maybe I will drop by and catch some of the talk, maybe I won't, depending on how the day is going. With these events on the calendar, we can at least know the event is happening, so decisions can be made as time approaches.

Why not put other things on the calendar? If we mix what is critical with what is optional, we can no longer see what is critical. When an opportunity arises, we must be able to take one look at the calendar and say yea or nay. We cannot do that if the three critical items are mixed in with the 57 that are not.

An Organized Task List

No one knows who originally thought up the idea of the to-do list. More than likely, as soon the first such list grew to more than about five items, the question arose, "How do I know which one to do right now?" Certainly, every one of us can generate a list of our obligations that far exceeds what can be accomplished by the end of the day. Having some way to organize a laundry list of tasks into a doable *game plan* is the challenge.

Make the Next Step Crystal Clear

Examine your own list. How many of those items really take a number of steps to complete? How many lack all the information necessary to accomplish them? How many of the tasks are simply ambiguous and leave you at a loss to where to begin? When someone looks at a list and sees two items—a difficult one and an easy one—human nature dictates choosing the easy one. *Buy shoestrings* wins out over *solve world hunger* every time because we know exactly how to go about buying shoestrings. Solving world hunger, like so many other goals we may have, is large and undefined. We really do not know where to begin.

The first rule of composing an organized task list is to make each task crystal clear. Figure 3.1 provides an example of a list where clear tasks are intermingled with goals that require multiple steps. Figure 3.2 provides a list that will actually stand a chance of being accomplished.

Figure 3.1. Unclear Task List

Supplies?
Improve math curriculum
Money for music program
Maintain computer
Orders?
Get summer school going

Figure 3.2. Crystal Clear Task List

Mills: Want to teach summer school?

Carter: Schedule observation

Room 102: Check on heat

Acme 555–8312: Check on status of order

Register for math workshop 555–7646

Run SpyBot

Research sources for music grants

Outline ABC report

Compose blog post in use of ALEX

What makes the tasks in Figure 3.2 *crystal clear*? They possess the following characteristics:

- Crystal clear tasks include verbs. Verbs are the *doing* part of speech. Read a crystal clear task and you know exactly what it is you are supposed to do. Clarifying what is to be done on the front end increases the chances that you will know what to do when you see that task on the list later in the week.

- Crystal clear tasks can be accomplished in one sitting and ideally can be accomplished in a few minutes. Overly burdensome tasks tend to sit idle on lists whereas those that are easy to do get done. The trick is to break big jobs into tasks that are small enough that they are accomplished in a short period of time.

- Crystal clear tasks have all needed information at hand. If the task is a phone call, the crystal clear task has the phone number already written down. The agenda for the phone call is already written out.

- Crystal clear tasks can be done now, without something else having to happen first. If something else must happen first, that is the task to appear on the list.

Group Items That Go Together

Much has been written about arranging tasks by priority and working on high-priority items first. Certainly, we all have tasks that are critical to accomplish today while others can wait. Over the long haul, however, concentrating on the few critical items and ignoring everything else eventually results in a large backlog of tasks.

The reality of our jobs is that much comes our way on a daily basis. The ability to handle large numbers of fairly small tasks is essential. In many cases, other people require our approval or input in some way before they can move forward on a project. If we are focused only on a few critical items, the danger is that we become a huge bottleneck and hinder the productivity of those around us.

To accomplish a large number of tasks as quickly as possible, group similar items and handle the whole group at one time. For example, rather than interrupt a colleague with a question, start a list of items to discuss with that person; and run through the entire list with that person during a single sitting. Rather than drive across town for one errand, start a list. When the list is long enough to make the trip worthwhile, run all the errands in a single trip.

Phone calls provide another opportunity to group similar items. List all the phone calls together. When you pick up a phone, crank through the whole list. You will spend less time on each call when you know another five must be made right after it.

The birthday card example from the last chapter provides a perfect example of grouping. We bought all the cards in a group, addressed them all in a group, and so forth, before dropping them into tickler files. Approving purchase orders, signing checks, or handling leave requests provide similar examples.

Suppose a principal wants to encourage student participation in an upcoming event. One way this could be accomplished is to make an announcement over the pubic address system each morning, with each announcement unique and building in excitement to the day of the event. The project should flow more smoothly if the principal blocks out some time and writes all the announcements in one group. The task then becomes picking a day for each announcement and dropping each in the appropriate tickler file.

Plan Weekly

Use the entire week as a canvas on which to create the following week. Too many people use tomorrow's list to house a month's worth of tasks. When tomorrow comes to an end, they rewrite 99% of those tasks again for the next day. The truth is most of the items on our list do not have to be accomplished on a particular day. Look at what you wish to accomplish during the coming week. Write them so they are crystal clear. Group similar items. The tasks you have identified can be accomplished quicker this way than in any other.

Using a loose-leaf planner provides the ability to add blank lined pages. An excellent time saver is to insert several pages between the two facing pages for the current day. At the end of the day, rather than recopy the items left undone, simply move the pages forward a day.

One simple idea for keeping the list readable and attractive throughout the week is to use a highlighter for completed items. The makers of the Time-Design system (www.timesystem.us) suggest this technique. If we mark through an item with a ballpoint pen, the item becomes unreadable and the list unattractive. Placing a check mark beside completed items keeps the appearance neat; however, the items still to be done do not easily stand out from those completed. Highlight items as you complete them, and they are still readable. The items that have not been highlighted stand out.

Work Ahead of Deadlines

When we are able to group similar tasks, those tasks are accomplished much faster than attacking them any other way. The greatest single enemy of this approach consists of working too close to deadlines. When deadlines loom, days are driven by whatever project is about to crash. Those who have waited too long to complete an application or request a purchase order have experienced what happens when the day is deadline driven. One winds up spending the better part of a day *walking* paperwork through its various steps, interrupting other people to ask them to act on the emergency, and experiencing a great deal of unneeded stress. Conversely, the exact same paperwork initiated a week ago would have required virtually no time. The paperwork would wind its way through the pipeline while the person spends time making headway on a variety of projects.

The focus of today must never be to simply complete what must be done today. The organized school leader stays ahead of the curve. If a project begins to bog down, enough time has been built in to compensate. Orders are placed with vendors so that they arrive in plenty of time. Tasks are delegated to others far enough in advance that the people to whom we delegate need not immediately drop their other initiatives to work on the new assignment.

Moving from a feeling of just keeping one's head above water to a feeling of being well ahead of deadlines may require extra time for a while. The process also entails taking a hard look at the list for things that can be postponed until much later as well as things that need not be done at all.

Delegation

From time to time, we assign a task to someone and want to be sure the other person comes through. We loan a book and want to be sure the book is returned. We order materials from a business and want to be sure that what we have ordered is delivered, the order is correct, and we have been charged the correct amount. Each scenario is an example of delegation. The task belongs to someone else, yet we have a vested interest in its completion. How can we keep track of all the tasks that belong to someone else?

The signature tool provides the answer. As soon as the assignment is made, as soon as the book is loaned, or as soon as the order is placed, a note goes in the signature tool. Delegated items can be classified items into three categories:

1. *Date specific*: The task must be completed by a certain day this week. For this type, flip to that day and make an entry. Part of one's responsibility when that day comes is to follow up as needed on that task.

2. *No specific date but should be completed within the next week*: I would certainly expect any phone message I leave to be returned within the week. The same exists for small tasks. Group these items together in a list. Friday is a good day to check the status of such items.

3. *Tasks that should be accomplished within the month*: An order placed may require several weeks for delivery. Reserve the page just behind the last day of the month in the back of the planner to list delegated items. Figure 3.3 shows a sample list of delegated items. Notice the parentheses used beside several items. Their use will become clear in the next section as we discuss documentation.

Figure 3.3, List of Delegated Tasks

Adams: Borrowed *Excellence in Teaching* book

Cooper: Minutes from grade-level meeting

Acme: Order #18762 (4/12)

Smith: Update on Billy Jones (4/21)

Documentation Made Simple

Every first-year teacher has been told documentation is important. Countless times during our careers, we are reminded to *document*. How many of us, however, have really been taught how to document? Exactly what is it that we are supposed to document? How do we know what is important and what is not? Where do we document? In practice, few people have a good ongoing system of documentation.

The key element for a person to document on a regular basis is that the system is *easy*. During my early years in education, I tried various approaches to documenting such tasks as telephone calls to parents, all without much success. No matter what I tried, the paperwork involved was just enough trouble to cause me to abandon the system. I credit a book entitled *Time Power* (Hobbs, 1987) with showing me an easy approach to documenting the events of the day. Finally, I had a system easy enough I would actually do it!

The standard Day-Timer or Franklin-Covey planner offer two facing pages for each day. The left-hand page houses appointments and tasks. The right-hand page provides a place for the type of documentation we will discuss. The same result can be accomplished with a loose-leaf binder and blank paper or a spiral notebook. A legal pad with a page devoted to each day is another option. The first few lines can be used to list appointments for the day, a large section in the middle reserved for the task list, and the bottom portion of the page and reverse side of the page provide ample space for documentation.

The page used for documentation replaces each of the following items:

◆ The notepad that lives by the phone

◆ The legal pad that accompanies us to the meeting

◆ The back of the scrap envelope we reach for to jot a quick note

◆ Post-its stuck everywhere

◆ The napkin in the purse left over from last night's dinner

◆ The grocery list stuck to the refrigerator door

In short, the documentation page provides a single place to capture anything we must record during the course of the day. At the end of the day, decide what needs to be done about what was written.

Here are some examples of what one might find during a day's documentation:

◆ You receive a call from a friend inviting you to a party. While he is giving relaying the date, time, instructions on what to bring, and directions on how to get there, jot it all in one place—today's documentation page. When the call is over, close the book and resume doing whatever it was you were doing, trusting that all the information has been captured in your planner.

◆ You order some materials over the phone. On the documentation page, jot the name of the person you spoke with, his or her extension, the order confirmation number, any discount promised, and other information that might be needed later.

- You normally go to the grocery store on Saturday afternoon, so Saturday's documentation page is the place to make the grocery list. Every time you think of something you need, flip to Saturday and jot it on that page.

- You have a conference scheduled with a parent. Every time you think of something to discuss, open the planner to the day of that conference and enter it on the documentation page. You are building an agenda as you go. During the conference, take notes on the documentation page.

- At the end of the day, mentally review the day and identify significant events. Perhaps an award is bestowed on you or your school. An event has taken place that moves forward a school or personal goal. This page provides a place to capture those bits of good news.

A quick review of that documentation page at the end of the day is vital in keeping the system alive. Look at what you have written throughout the day on today's documentation and ask yourself, "What does this mean to me?" or "When will I need to see this again?"

The first example was an invitation to a party. When looking at those notes at the end of the day, they are your cue to flip to the appropriate day in your planner and note the party on the appropriate time slot. You also see from your notes that there are a few items you are to bring. Flip to Saturday's page and jot on the task list a couple of items you need to buy at the grocery store.

On the day of the party, how are you going to remember what to bring? How are you going to remember how to get there? Here is the real magic of your documentation page—being able to go right back to information exactly when you need it.

Suppose the conversation about the party happened on May 10. As you review your notes at the end of the day, turn in your planner to the day it is going to occur and write "Party" by the correct time slot. Put out beside it this notation: (5/10). Anything in parentheses in your planner tells you, "Go to this date for more information." When it is time to leave for the party, that little note that says "(5/10)" tells you to look back in your planner to May 10. You are now looking at the notes you took on that date, and hence looking at a list of what to bring and directions on how to get there!

We have talked about taking notes on the documentation page when placing orders by phone. When the call is over, your documentation is over. At the end of the day, look at your notes and ask yourself what would be a reasonable amount of time to allow for the order to arrive. Flip ahead in your planner and in the to-do section write, "Acme (5/10)." When that date arrives, that entry sends you back in your planner to May 10, the day you placed the order with Acme. When you call to check on the order, you are equipped with the phone number with extension, the name of the person spoken with, the confirmation number, and all other needed information at your fingertips.

This next scenario is common: the principal taking notes during a call from a parent and following through with the action required. The administrative assistant hands you one of those little pink slips of paper that says John Smith's father has called. You return the call; and while on the phone, you take some notes. Do not write down everything that is said, but instead simply jot down the important points. If the date is October 25th, you are going to be writing on documentation page for October 25th. During the conversation, jot down the name. Beside the name, jot the phone number. Now, throw away that little pink slip of paper!

The father tells you about the problem. He says that other students are picking on his son during math class. Suppose you tell him you will talk to the teacher, explaining that she may not even be aware this is going on. You also promise to call him back in 2 weeks to see if the problem has been resolved. During the course of the conversation, Mr. Smith rambles a bit and tells you about the house in which the family will be moving and even tells you where it is located. While he talks, you continue to jot a few notes. When the phone call is over, the documentation is over. Now, let us take a look at what you might have written in the planner as illustrated in Figure 3.4.

Figure 3.4. Example of Documentation

Oct. 25

John Smith: 362–1234

Father called. Says other students are picking on him in math class.

✳ Talk to teacher.

✳ Call him back in 2 weeks to ask about progress.

Are moving into new house this weekend. Directions: Head north on main street. Turn right on Maple. 3rd house on left.

Notice that during the conversation, you created two to-do items for yourself:

1. Talk to teacher.
2. Call Mr. Smith back in 2 weeks.

The asterisk is my symbol that what is written is not just information but is something requiring action on my part. The tasks for today consist of what is in the task list on the left-hand page along with anything on the documentation page with an asterisk beside it.

You could probably talk to the teacher that same day and complete that task. Here is how you to handle the second point, that of calling Mr. Smith 2 weeks later. Flip ahead two weeks in the planner and on the task list, write what is shown in Figure 3.5. Close the planner and forget all about Mr. Smith. He is off your mind.

Figure 3.5. Task Referring Back to Documentation

Call Mr. Smith (10/25)

Two weeks later, you open your planner and see "Call Mr. Smith" in the task list. The notation "(10/25)" tells you to look at October 25th. Anything in parentheses in the planner means *look here for more information*. Flip back to October 25th and you are suddenly back to the notes made during that conversation. The name, the phone number, a summary of the conversation, and the commitments made during that conversation are all there.

While returning the call to Mr. Smith, look at the notes taken 2 weeks ago. Although you may not have given those notes or that conversation another moment's thought since the original conversation, you are able to demonstrate a good grasp of what was discussed. You are also establishing a reputation with this man of being someone who can follow through on commitments.

During the conversation, you might also say, "By the way, how are things coming with the new house? Let me see if I remember what you had told me. If I go down Main Street and take a right on Maple, isn't it the third house on the left?" Mr. Smith will think you have a great memory! Maybe you do have a good memory. Maybe you just have a good system. Mr. Smith never needs to know the difference!

Opportunities such as this one occur frequently. We place an order on the telephone and it does not come as expected. All too often, the conversation sounds something like this: "This is Penelope Jones and I talked to somebody there about ordering some stuff and it's been a long time and it still hasn't come."

Why did the conversation sound the way it did? Perhaps Penelope simply did not document at all during the phone call. Perhaps she took careful notes, but they were on the back of a scrap envelope that is now nowhere to be found.

What if Penelope had used the technique outlined in this chapter? During the call, she would have jotted down the name of the business and the phone number. She would have also written the name of the salesman and his extension number. When he gave her the order number, she would write that down as well. She would also make a note about the 15% discount he promised her. Finally, she records that the salesman has promised the order will arrive in 10 business days.

When Penelope gets off the phone, she flips ahead 2 weeks on her planner and writes "Acme Inc." In parentheses, she writes today's date. Penelope may now close the planner and forget all about Acme. Two weeks later, she will see a reminder in her task list concerning this order. If the order has not arrived, Penelope will be on the telephone. This time, however, the conversation will be different:

> Could I speak to Sam Johnson at extension 718? Hi Sam, this is Penelope Jones. I am calling about order number 54321, which I placed on March 15th. You had said it would arrive within 10 business days and now it has been 15 business days and it still has not come. Could you check on the status of that order for me? The amount will be how much? Sam, you specifically told me I would get a 15% discount. I wrote that down in my planner when we talked.

No one is going to argue when you are armed this type of information, and you are sure to get better service.

Monthly Index

In the example with Mr. Smith and Penelope, information was written on the documentation page indicating exactly when it was needed again. What about the information that you may need again, but don't know when? For example, you order a printer and speak with a particularly helpful salesman. Six months later, you need to order another printer and wish you could put your hands on the notes from that conversation. You teach secondary school and have 150 students. You hold a parent conference and jot notes on the documentation page. Six months later, you need to find your notes from that conference. How do you put your hands on them? There is no need to thumb through all of those pages looking for that information. A little ritual, which requires approximately 20 minutes at the end of each month, allows any piece of information to be found in seconds by simply using the find command on Microsoft Word.

This monthly index consists of one Microsoft Word file. Each month consists of a single paragraph of text and numbers. At first glance, the index appears to be nothing more than gibberish. Each month, open that document, scroll to the end, and enter information for the next month. Figure 3.6 gives an example of the finished product for a typical month.

Figure 3.6. Example of Monthly Index

May 2008
1. Barber Sale, Dodd, BCI Jane
2. Sue Smith top prize
5. Cookie dough salesman Jones, Milkbox repair
6. Montgomery IEP
7. Baker teacher complaint, Student Council field trip
9. Burns SYETP
12. Order printer MicroLowPrice
13. Pizza Hut compliment
14. Jones DHR attorney, Tate late, Donald Jones painter
15. Jeremy Davis conference retention
16. House paint
19. PowerPrint registered
20. XYA registration number
22. Sungate Records
27. Yearbook meeting
28. Copier lease
29. Manuscript mailed, ethics meeting

To add a new month to the index, simply sit down at the computer with the planner. Look at the documentation for the first day of the month, key in a *1* and add a key word or two for any item on that date that is of *lasting value*. For example, May 1, 2008, has three entries that might need to be reference again. One involved a company called *Barber Sales*, another involving someone named *Dodd*, and a third involving Jane at a company called *BCI*. Continue the process each day in the month. Generally, the entire process can be completed in 20 minutes.

Just above this block of text is a similar block for April 2008. Just below it is a block for June 2008. The entire monthly index, which may extend several years into the past, is housed in one Microsoft Word file.

When looking for a particular piece of information, all you do is open that one Word document. Use the *find* command and enter a key word. The software will land on each occurrence of that term. In just a few seconds, you can find the piece of information you need.

The following example illustrates how this procedure works. A principal talks with a salesman at a particular company and orders a printer. During the conversation, the principal writes the name of the company, the salesman, the phone number, order confirmation number, exactly what was being ordered, the price, any discount, and any other pertinent information. When the conversation ends, the principal flips ahead a couple of weeks in the planner and makes an entry in the task list as a reminder to follow up if the order is not received as expected. Parentheses containing today's date point him back to all the notes taken during the conversation. The order arrives on schedule, and he checks off the task as *done*.

Six months later, the principal wants to add an additional printer at the school. He remembers the helpful salesman and the reasonable price. If only he could put his hands on his notes, the principal could easily reach that same company and salesman. The monthly index allows one to do just that.

The principal opens the document and enlists the help of the *find* command. What key term might he use? *Printer* comes to mind, so he enters the word *printer* in the search window. The search lands on the term in the midst of the entry that says, "12. Order printer MicroLowPrice" (Figure 3.6). This line was a part of the May 2008 paragraph. The principal can go back to the documentation taken during May 2008. Specifically, he turns to May 10, 2008. The notes taken during that conversation are now in front of him. He now has the telephone number for the company as well as the name and extension for the particular salesman who helped him and all the details from that conversation.

Every day, we are involved in phone calls and conferences with parents. At the time of the conversation, we have little clue as to need for any documentation. The conversation may simply be routine. Conversely, what seemed like a routine conversation may erupt into a volatile situation several weeks later. You never know when you might need your documentation.

Most of what is documented will never be accessed again. Therefore, we do not want to spend a great deal of time in the documentation process. Take a few notes while you are on the phone or in conference. When the conversation is over, the documentation is over. Twenty minutes at the end of the month ensures that you can put your hands on any documentation whenever you need it. That is easy enough you might actually do it!

Future Tasks

Obviously, not every task you set out for yourself will be accomplished during the coming week. We all need someplace to trap the tasks that need to be done but are not expected to get done this week.

In the back of the planner, label a page *Future Tasks* and use that page to list any new task that comes your way but will not be completed this week. Depending on the number of tasks, several pages may be required. One could be devoted to tasks for later this month, one for tasks to be accomplished the next month, and so forth.

Next Steps

- Look at your current to-do or task list. After reading this chapter, do you see problems with your list? Can you rewrite the tasks to make them clearer and more doable?

- Before making a firm decision on what to use as your signature tool, read Chapter 4. Then give serious thought to which tool best suits your needs: a paper-based or a digital system.

- If your decision is paper, make a trip to your local office supply store and look at the selection of planners available for purchase. Remember, the major functions your tool must handle are calendar items, tasks, and documentation. Also remember that your signature tool is one that will be with you everywhere you go.

- If your choice for a signature tool is digital, go ahead and establish a monthly index on your computer now, even before you have anything to enter into it. Merely establishing the index is the first step toward adding to it each month.

Enter a task for the last day of this month reminding you to update your monthly index. Do the same for the next couple of months. After reading Chapter 5, you may want your *repeating task list* to handle this reminder for you.

4

Your Signature Tool: Organizing Digitally

There's not enough time in the day. Our enemy is time, and technology is the only way [to combat that].

John Q. Porter,
District Administration Magazine, June 2006

Soon after desktop computers became common, software allowing for the maintenance of calendars, to-do lists, and addresses quickly appeared. These programs afforded the user to change a date, move forward an uncompleted task, or update a telephone number without rewriting, making them intriguing alternatives to paper-based systems. The advent of handheld computers has led many people to turn to technology as a means of keeping track of the details in their lives.

This chapter explores a thought process to help you decide if a *digital signature tool* is the right decision for you. The chapter also provides a methodology for how to use this digital signature tool to organize your life. The marketplace offers a variety of makes and models of these tools, each accompanied by an owner's manual outlining the basics of how to operate the device. What is sorely lacking is the methodology for how to use the device. Although each passing year brings new models offering more features, the strategies offered here continue to be sound.

A Day in the Life . . .

Perhaps the easiest way to illustrate the advantages of digitally organizing is to shadow a school leader who does so. The following is a day in the life of Jim, principal of Anytown Middle School. Jim's varied and extensive use of his signature tool may not be typical. However, his day does illustrate the many possibilities handheld tools offer.

5:30 AM	Jim normally awakens to his alarm clock, but the alarm began to malfunction a couple of days ago. Jim simply set the alarm on his digital signature tool and is awakened promptly at 5:30.
6:00 AM	Jim is about to walk out the door and had all but forgotten today is trash day. It is a good thing he set a repeating alarm to remind him to roll the trash receptacle to the curb.
6:10 AM	Jim is sitting at his favorite breakfast spot. While he sips on a cup of coffee, he reads e-mail messages that have arrived since leaving work yesterday. Several messages are from a Listserv for school administrators to which he belongs. Jim finds the Listserv an effective way to ask for input from colleagues around the country.
6:13 AM	The school chorus is traveling to a competition this morning, so Jim uses his signature tool to make a quick phone call to the transportation department. The voice at the other end assures Jim the buses will arrive on time. He sends a quick e-mail to the choral director with this information and wishes her luck in the competition.
6:17 AM	Jim's breakfast is served. Having already double-checked on the trip, he is able to relax and enjoy his meal.
6:47 AM	After arriving in his office, Jim boots his computer and plugs a cable into his signature tool. The few changes made on his handheld device since leaving the office yesterday are now synchronized with Microsoft Outlook on his desktop computer.

6:51 AM	Jim looks at his task list. Because he tries to work ahead of deadlines, few tasks are urgent. His aim is to organize tasks so that like tasks are grouped together. The list is sorted by date due, so some creative reassignment of due dates groups his tasks. He assigns a due date of 5 days ago to a half dozen tasks he can complete before students arrive. He sees another half dozen he can accomplish while in the hallways before homeroom begins. He assigns a due date of 4 days ago to them. Several phone calls are next and receive a due date of 3 days ago. As each task is assigned a new due date, the task jumps to its new place on the list.
6:57 AM	Jim is now looking at a list of doable tasks for the day arranged in groups of similar tasks. He now has a plan for the day and synchronizes with his signature tool once again, giving him the same organized tasks list on the handheld device.
7:10 AM	Jim makes himself visible in the halls as buses arrive. His early morning group of tasks includes a quick conversation with the lunchroom manager and two teachers whom he will see as they arrive. He will also check the status of several maintenance items listed on his handheld.
7:20 AM	Jim's signature tool rings. His administrative assistant is calling and needs to know if Jim can meet with a fellow principal this afternoon. Jim has his calendar stored on his handheld, quickly checks his schedule, adds the new appointment, and asks the administrative assistant to confirm the meeting.
7:50 AM	Jim returns to the office to make the morning announcements via the public address system.
7:55 AM	Jim tells his administrative assistant he will be conducting a classroom observation. He leaves the office with his signature tool and a small keyboard.
8:00 AM	Jim begins his observation in an eighth-grade algebra class. He takes notes on his signature tool attached to a small keyboard.

8:45 AM	Jim returns to the office. As he synchronizes the handheld, the notes taken during the observation are transferred to Microsoft Outlook. He copies the notes and pastes them into the official observation instrument. He adds the finishing touches to the instrument and e-mails a copy of the observation to the teacher. The e-mail also suggests a time the following day that they might meet for the postobservation conference.
9:00 AM	Jim turns his attention to e-mail that has arrived during the morning. One message is from the superintendent and announces a meeting at an off-site location. The message includes driving directions for how to get to the meeting and outlines the agenda. Jim uses Microsoft Outlook's drag and drop capability to drag the e-mail to his calendar. He assigns a date and time. Before closing the appointment, he sets an alarm to remind him of the appointment 30 minutes ahead of its start time. Jim can rest assured that he will not forget the meeting. The alarm on his signature tool will not let him forget. When he gets in the car, the driving directions will be safely tucked away in a note attached to the meeting on his signature tool. The agenda will go with him, being stored in that same note.
9:02 AM	Another e-mail requests some statistical information. Jim forwards this e-mail to the administrative assistant and annotates it with a request that she handle the request. He includes himself in the BCC (blind courtesy [carbon] copy) line of the e-mail. The next time Microsoft Outlook downloads e-mail, the copy that arrives in his Inbox serves as a reminder of the task he has delegated.
9:03 AM	Another e-mail advertises a free webinar. Jim is not sure if he wants to register, but he wants to see the invitation again in a week. He drags the e-mail to his task list and assigns both a start date and due date a week from now. Jim can now delete the e-mail and forget about the invitation. A week from now, the invitation will show up on his task list. All the details will be in a note attached to the task.

9:30 AM	Jim receives a call from a parent who is upset about something that took place in her child's class. As he listens Jim turns to his computer and opens a new task. He takes notes in the large space designated for notes. When the conversation ends, he decides what action he needs to take. He decides he will drop by the teacher's room after school. In the task line he types the teacher's name and a few keywords. The next time he synchronizes his handheld, he will have the notes from the phone call at his fingertips as he discusses the matter with the teacher.
10:45 AM	Jim goes to the cafeteria. The first lunch wave is 15 minutes away, so the room is unusually quiet. He uses these few minutes to check the voice mail on his handheld and to call his office voicemail. He is able to quickly return three calls generated from those messages. One of the calls he places is an order for teaching materials. The receptionist asks for his account number. The contact list on Jim's signature tool has ample room to record such information. Jim is able to look up the account number during the call.
1:00 PM	Jim attends a meeting with his Parent-Teacher Association Board. They ask if he will start the meeting with an inspiring message. The notepad feature of his signature tool provides the perfect place to store such reference information. He quickly pulls up a story he discovered on the Internet some months ago that he thought would be perfect for occasions such as this.
1:45 PM	Glancing at today's newspaper, Jim sees the dates of upcoming symphony concerts. He is particularly interested in the pops concert coming up in a month. "I wonder if they have their program selections for that concert posted on the web site," Jim thinks. He goes to the site and finds the complete list of selections that will be played, along with other details about the evening's performance. He clicks and drags the mouse to highlight the desired information and uses the copy command. Turning to Microsoft Outlook, Jim enters the date of the concert on his calendar. He pastes all the information copied from the web site into the note section of that appointment. When he leaves from work today, all the information will be available to him on his signature tool.

3:00 PM	Jim supervises bus dismissal. One of the buses is not in the lineup, so Jim makes a quick call to the transportation office from his signature tool.
3:30 PM	Jim stops by the textbook storage room to check for surplus books. The power goes out, and without windows in the storage room, Jim finds himself in total darkness. Jim pulls out his signature tool and presses a key. The light from the handheld provides enough illumination for Jim to find the door. "All these features and it's a flashlight too!" he thinks.
3:45 PM	Jim's wife calls to tell him she has volunteered the two of them to become members of a supper club. It will meet at 6:00 PM the second Saturday of every month. As he listens, Jim enters the appointment into Microsoft Outlook, clicks on *recurrence*, and selects monthly and second Saturday as the pattern. The supper club will now show up every month without another entry being made.
5:00 PM	Jim synchronizes his signature tool with Microsoft Outlook once again. He walks out the door empty-handed; yet in his pocket is a very complete calendar, an organized task list, his entire address book, a wealth of reference material, the ability to make a phone call, and even a quasiflashlight, all in one little tool.

The intent of this *day-in-the-life* example is twofold. First, for someone with no background, the versatility of this tool is clear. Jim's story may be the spark to motivate a novice to learn more about the capabilities. Second, for someone who is familiar with devices such as the Palm or BlackBerry, Jim's day will likely provide ideas for their use.

Paper or Digital:
Three Recommendations for Making the Choice

If you are contemplating moving from a paper system to a digital one, Jim's day illustrates many advantages of the latter. To help with making that decision, consider these three recommendations:

Experiment With a Handheld Device

Get the feel of the digital device by taking a trip to a local office supply store and a couple of cell phone retailers. The variety of models available and the ever-changing nature of the industry prevent offering any type of meaningful tutorial here. A helpful sales person should be able to show you how to navigate the device to add appointments or tasks. Also, any book superstore carries books that explain how to work the device.

Experiment With the Desktop Software

Second, experiment with the software you will use to synchronize with the handheld device. Microsoft Outlook is so common that any handheld that has the capability to synchronize with any type of desktop software can synchronize with Microsoft Outlook. Because Microsoft Outlook is a standard component of Microsoft Office, the program is already accessible to most school leaders. The Palm user has a second option, synchronizing with the Palm Desktop. This software can be downloaded from Palm's web site for free. Because Microsoft Outlook is such a widely used program, manufacturers tend build in capabilities allowing their products to synchronize with it. Both the Palm handheld and the BlackBerry synchronize with Microsoft Outlook.

Examine How Much Information Arrives Digitally

Finally, examine how much information arrives digitally. How many e-mails do you receive that include directions on how to get to a destination, agendas for meetings, confirmations of online orders, or requests from others to perform certain tasks? How much information do you acquire from the Internet? In each case printing the information to paper is one answer. However, the process only makes the problem of the glut of paper in our lives that much worse. A much better alternative is to develop a system that allows information that arrives digitally to stay digital.

The Appendix provides detailed instructions on how to configure Microsoft Outlook. The body of this chapter discusses the methodology of how to use Microsoft Outlook and your signature tool. If you are new to Microsoft Outlook, or if at any point some aspect of using Microsoft Outlook is unclear, please refer to the Appendix for direction.

The Calendar

As with the paper calendar, clarity is key. The calendar should display exactly three types of items:

1. Appointments: Assign a start and end time. Set an alarm if necessary. If the same appointment recurs regularly, enter that information. Use the note section to add details about the appointment. The meeting called by Jim's superintendent in his e-mail is such an example (Figure 4.1). When synchronized to the handheld device, the appointment and all the notes will transfer. Figure 4.2 shows the results of what will happen when the computer is synchronized to a handheld device. The icon to the right of the appointment shows that notes are attached.

Figure 4.1. Appointment With Information in Note Section

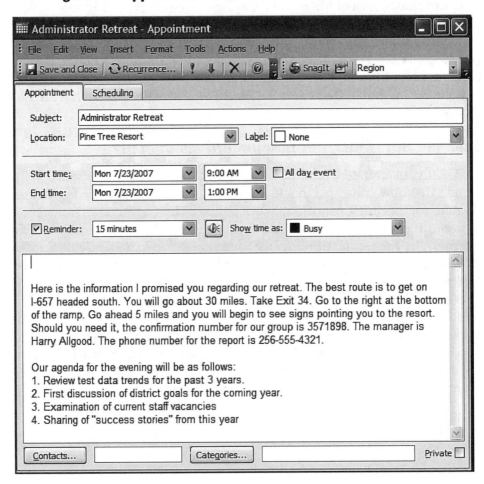

Figure 4.2. Appointment With Notes on Handheld

2. Tasks that absolutely must be done that day: Reserve time on the calendar and treat working on that task as you would any other appointment.

3. Events and activities that should be known about the day: If no particular time is associated with the event, make it an *All-Day Event* as explained in the Appendix. The All-Day Event handles such situations as these:

   • School holidays. For holidays that extend beyond a day, create one All-Day Event and simply indicate the start and end date. The event banner appears on each day included in the range.

   • Ending dates of grading periods or dates report cards are to be sent.

   • Standardized test date windows. These time frames are published statewide more than a year in advance. Having them on the calendar helps greatly when planning the school year.

An additional use for the All-Day Event is to record major accomplishments of the day. What history-making event occurred today? What milestone occurred in your personal or professional life? Recording these types of events provides a permanent record of the most significant happenings in a person's life and time.

Microsoft Outlook also provides the capability of double-clicking on an All-Day Event and adding extensive notes. For example, the school's professional development days can be marked on the calendar. As plans are finalized for those days, record the details by double-clicking the All-Day Event banner and recording the details for the day (Figure 4.3).

Figure 4.3. All-Day Event With Notes

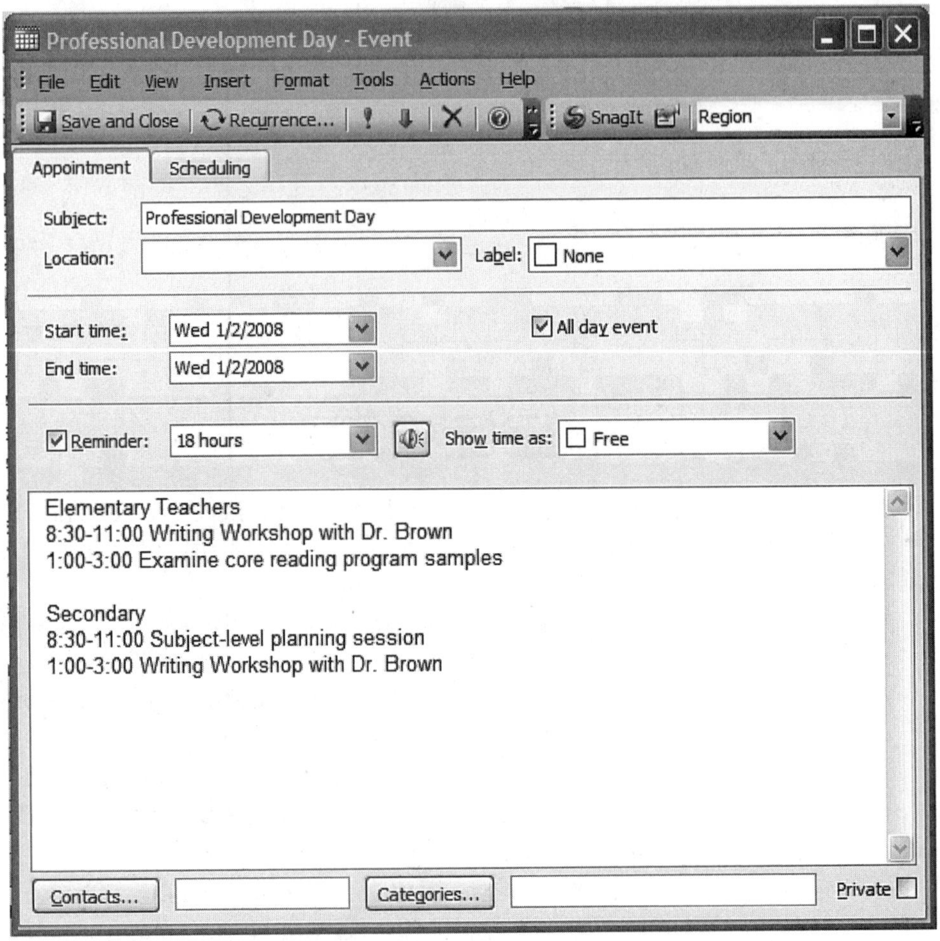

Other Calendar Views

One advantage of a paper month-at-a-glance style calendar is that it shows the *big picture*; a day-at-a-glance version provides room to write details. The Microsoft Outlook calendar provides both views. The user is not forced to choose between one of the other as with the paper calendar. The previous section illustrated the *1-Day* view. Buttons on the toolbar allow users to see the 5-day work week, the 7-day week, or the entire month. The ability to toggle between the 1-day and the monthly views provides a significant advantage for the busy school leader who must balance the big picture and the small details.

Both the Palm and BlackBerry allow the user to switch between a view of the day, week, or entire month. The month view uses dots to show the approximate position of appointments during the day—morning, afternoon, and evening. Figure 4.4 shows a month for which the 3rd has an appointment in the morning, the 7th has appointments in the morning and late afternoon, and the 14th has appointments covering all portions of the day. At a glance it is clear which days are open for appointments and which days are already committed. Clicking on any day immediately displays a detailed view of that day.

Figure 4.4. Appointments Shown in Monthly View

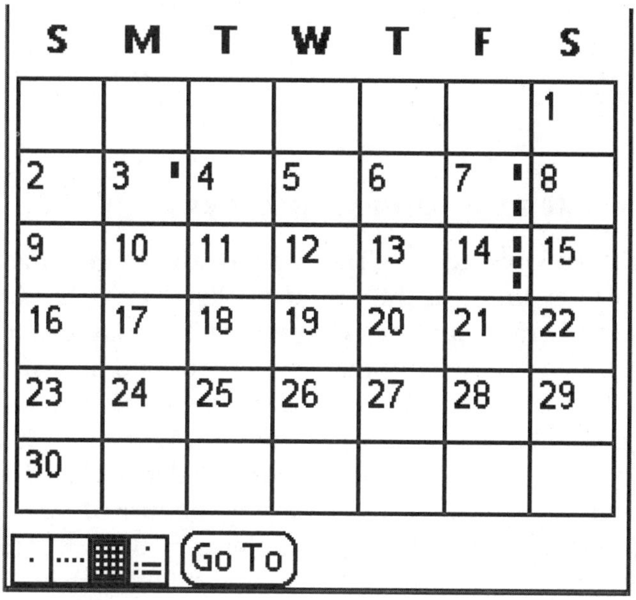

S	M	T	W	T	F	S
						1
2	3 ∎	4	5	6	7 ∎	8
9	10	11	12	13	14 ┇	15
16	17	18	19	20	21	22
23	24	25	26	27	28	29
30						

· ···· ▦ ⋮≡ (Go To)

Purging and Printing

Every few months, print the Microsoft Outlook monthly view for the last several months. This practice provides a *bird's-eye view* of one's life. On these calendars, restrict what is included to the major events and dates that are significant personally, professionally, or historically.

For this reason, routine repeating appointments or meetings that held little significance are deleted before printing. Minutes from those meetings are recorded elsewhere anyway. The perfect time to review the calendar, delete the insignificant, and polish the important is during waiting time. When waiting in a checkout line, in a doctor's office, or when stopped by a train, editing past days on the handheld calendar puts wasted time to work.

An Organized Task List

The real *meat* of this system is the organized task list. Imagine for a moment a to-do list that never requires rewriting. Imagine being able to jot down a task just one time and seeing that task reappear each week, each month, or each year without having to enter another thing. Imagine a to-do list where any item can be opened to reveal a world of background information. Finally, imagine a list that is easily searchable, allowing you to find any item in seconds. The Microsoft Outlook TaskPad is just such a tool. The Appendix provides details on how to structure the TaskPad for this system.

The organized task list on Microsoft Outlook adheres to the same principles as the one on paper examined in the last chapter:

- ◆ Word tasks clearly.
- ◆ Group similar items.
- ◆ Plan the list on a weekly basis.

Group Similar Items by Using *Due Dates*

Sort the TaskPad by due date. The obvious advantage is that it puts items that are about to expire near the top of the list. Due dates are also key in grouping related items. Suppose today is the 15th day of the month. The TaskPad may show several items that are overdue and have due dates of the 12th, 13th, or 14th. Perhaps a dozen tasks have a due date of the 15th and another dozen each have a due date of the 16th, 17th, and 18th. It is wise to allow some *breathing room* when assigning due dates. Due dates should be somewhat relative. A school leader's day can be turned upside down by a single emergency. If a report must be completed by the 18th, assigning a due date of the 18th is asking for trouble. A due date of the 14th or 15th allows for the possibility of the unexpected.

The best approach to the TaskPad is to organize the list in such a way that the most is accomplished in the shortest amount of time. Grouping related tasks accomplishes exactly that. Because the list automatically sorts by due date, related tasks can easily be grouped by reassigning due dates. All the tasks in one group have the same due date and therefore appear together.

Although today is the 15th, the five or six tasks that go together well at the very beginning of the day may receive a due date of the 1st of the month. The next group of tasks are assigned a due date of the 2nd of the month. In just a couple minutes, you can line up 50 tasks that can realistically be accomplish accomplish during the day, all organized in groups of three to six items each. Figure 4.5 shows an example of an organized task list on Microsoft Outlook. Figure 4.6 shows the same list on a handheld device.

Figure 4.5. Organized Task List in Outlook

☑	!	TaskPad	S.	Due Date	S...	N...	↻
		Click here to add a new Task					
☐		Write recommendation for Cameron	T.	Tue 5/1/2007	N...		
☐		PDWeb-Approve outstanding requests	T.	Tue 5/1/2007	N...		
☐		PDWeb-Monitor signup for Tim	T.	Tue 5/1/2007	N...		
☐		DC-How many licenses do we need for HTM ...	W	Wed 5/2/2...	N...		
☐		DC-Has money been approved for math inte...	W	Wed 5/2/2...	N...		
☐		DC-Status of order for student response sys...	T.	Thu 5/3/2007	N...		
☐		John-Discuss order for student response sys...	F.	Fri 5/4/2007	N...		
☐		John-Discuss rollover on STI program	F.	Fri 5/4/2007	N...		
☐		Blog-Post info on field day at elementary sch...	S.	Sat 5/5/2007	N...		
☐		Blog-Post info on Riley scholarship	S.	Sat 5/5/2007	N...		
☐		Balanced scorecard-Cut/paste summary of w...	S.	Sun 5/6/2007	N...		
☐		Balanced scorecard-Add DIBELS scores	S.	Sun 5/6/2007	N...		
☐		Ellis-Bailey-Any negative comments on math ...	M.	Mon 5/7/2007	N...		
☐		Ellis-Examine documentation for School Impr...	M.	Mon 5/7/2007	N...		
☐		Ellis-See counselor re: 7th grade orientation	M.	Mon 5/7/2007	N...		
☐		Ellis-Borrow software for interactive whitebo...	M.	Mon 5/7/2007	N...		
☐		JP-Call to set date to review writing continuum	T.	Tue 5/8/2007	N...		
☐		Set dates for SACS planning meetings for th...	T.	Tue 5/8/2007	N...		
☐		Set date to compose science pacing guides	T.	Tue 5/8/2007	N...		
☐		Jones-Borrowed 3 books	F.	Fri 5/18/2007	W...		

Figure 4.6. Organized Task List on Handheld

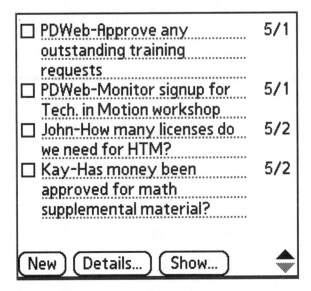

```
☐ PDWeb-Approve any          5/1
  outstanding training
  requests
☐ PDWeb-Monitor signup for   5/1
  Tech. in Motion workshop
☐ John-How many licenses do  5/2
  we need for HTM?
☐ Kay-Has money been         5/2
  approved for math
  supplemental material?

( New ) ( Details... ) ( Show... )   ▲
                                     ▼
```

Make Tasks Disappear and Reappear Using Start Dates

Some tasks cannot or should not be accomplished until a future date. School leaders constantly think of tasks needing attention during the following semester or summer. Certainly, these items, which do not require action until far in the future, need not clutter the list for today. By simply setting a start date for sometime in the future, those tasks are out of sight for now. They magically show up on the dates specified long ago.

Delegation

When a leader delegates a task to someone else, it is important to have the capability to follow through and see that the task is completed. Microsoft Outlook provides a field called *status*, which contains a choice called *waiting for someone else*. Changing the status of the task and assigning a due date brings that task back to the user's attention on the due date. It is also easy to see a list of all the tasks where someone else holds responsibility. Simply click the header on the *status* column and *waiting for someone else* tasks are grouped together on the list.

There is one caveat to this process. Be sure that any field used in Microsoft Outlook is also supported by with the same field on your signature tool. For example, as this book goes to press, the BlackBerry has the *status* field, whereas the Palm does not. Palm users can create a category called *waiting for* or *delegated*. When a task is delegated to someone else, the category is then changed.

Documentation Made Simple

In a digital system, the note section of a task is the place for documentation. When Jim fielded the parent call at 9:30, he opened a new task as soon as he picked up the telephone. He first entered notes from the conversation in the large block. Once the conversation was over, he had to decide what to do about the notes and when. At that point he completed the subject line and due date (Figure 4.7).

Figure 4.7. Documentation Taken During a Phone Call

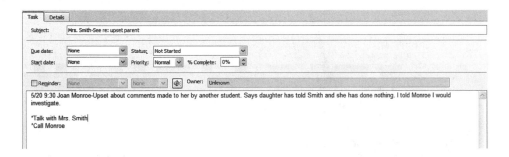

Keeping Digital Information Digital With Microsoft Outlook

In today's world, the school leader receives a flood of information via e-mail. A large part of staying afloat involves organizing digital information in a digital fashion. The *drag and drop* feature of Microsoft Outlook allows us to turn an e-mail into an appointment.

Drag and Drop E-mails to Make Them Appointments

At 9:00 Jim handled an e-mail from his superintendent that announced a meeting. Rather than print the e-mail and keep up with the printout of the driving directions and agenda, Jim chose to keep digital information digital. He closed the e-mail. He then clicked on the e-mail and dragged it over the Calendar button (Figure 4.8) where Microsoft Outlook opened a new appointment. We actually saw the results of this action on Figure 4.1. The subject of the e-mail automatically populated the subject line of the appointment. The body of the e-mail was duplicated in the note section of the appointment. All Jim had to do was set the date, set the time, and save the appointment. He can now delete the e-mail.

Figure 4.8. E-mail Being Dragged to the Calendar Button

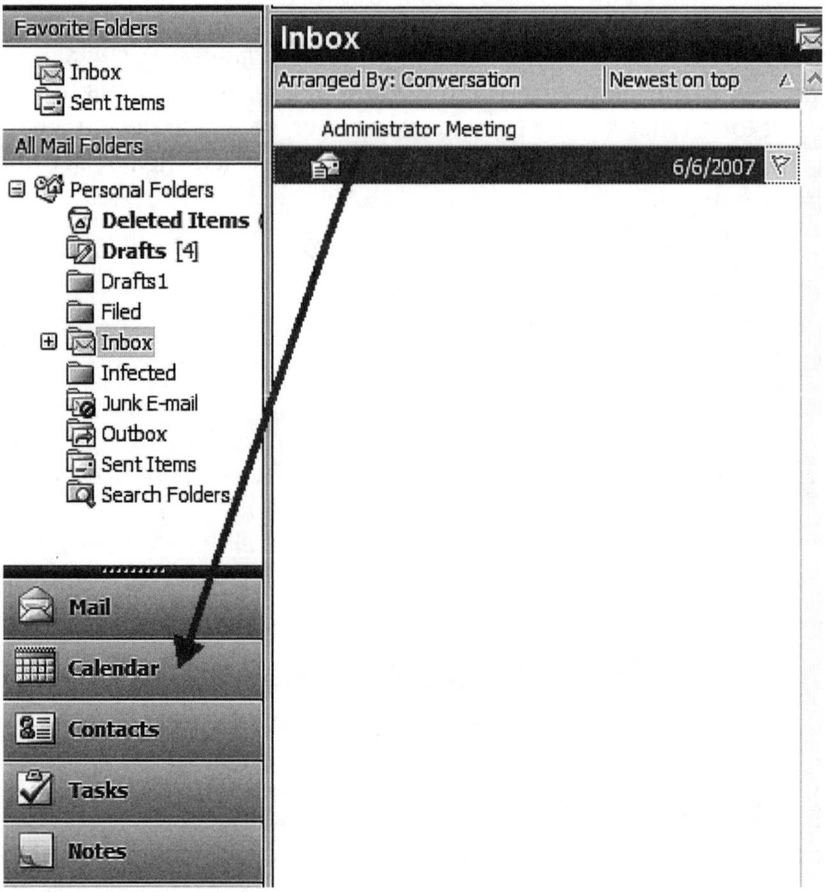

As soon as the mouse button is released, a new appointment form opens. The subject of the e-mail has become the title of this appointment. The entire body of the e-mail appears in the note section of the appointment. Simply select starting and ending dates and times for the appointment, set the alarm, and click Save and Close. The whole process takes only a few seconds and does not require the writing or printing a anything. The next time the handheld device is synchronized with Microsoft Outlook, this meeting (complete with the agenda and driving directions) is also on the handheld.

When time approaches to leave for the meeting, an alarm sounds both on Microsoft Outlook and on the handheld device as a reminder just in case the user has become preoccupied. Not sure how to get to the destination? The directions, which were originally a part of the e-mail, are on the handheld in a little note attached to that appointment. Likewise the meeting agenda, which was also part of the e-mail, is part of the note attached to that appointment.

Drag and Drop E-mails to Make Them Tasks

Many an e-mail embeds a to-do. We can drag and drop any e-mail and turn it into a task. During Jim's typical day, he received an e-mail inviting him to participate in a webinar. He really does not know at this point if he wants to participate but feels that within a week he can make a decision. Basically, Jim wants this information to go away and reappear in a week. He closes the e-mail. He then proceeds to click and drag the e-mail over the Task button (Figure 4.9). Microsoft Outlook opens a new task (Figure 4.10). The subject of the e-mail automatically populates the subject line of the task, and the body of the e-mail is duplicated in the task's note section. All Jim has to do is set the start and due dates and save the task. He can now delete the e-mail.

Figure 4.9. E-mail Being Dragged to Task Button

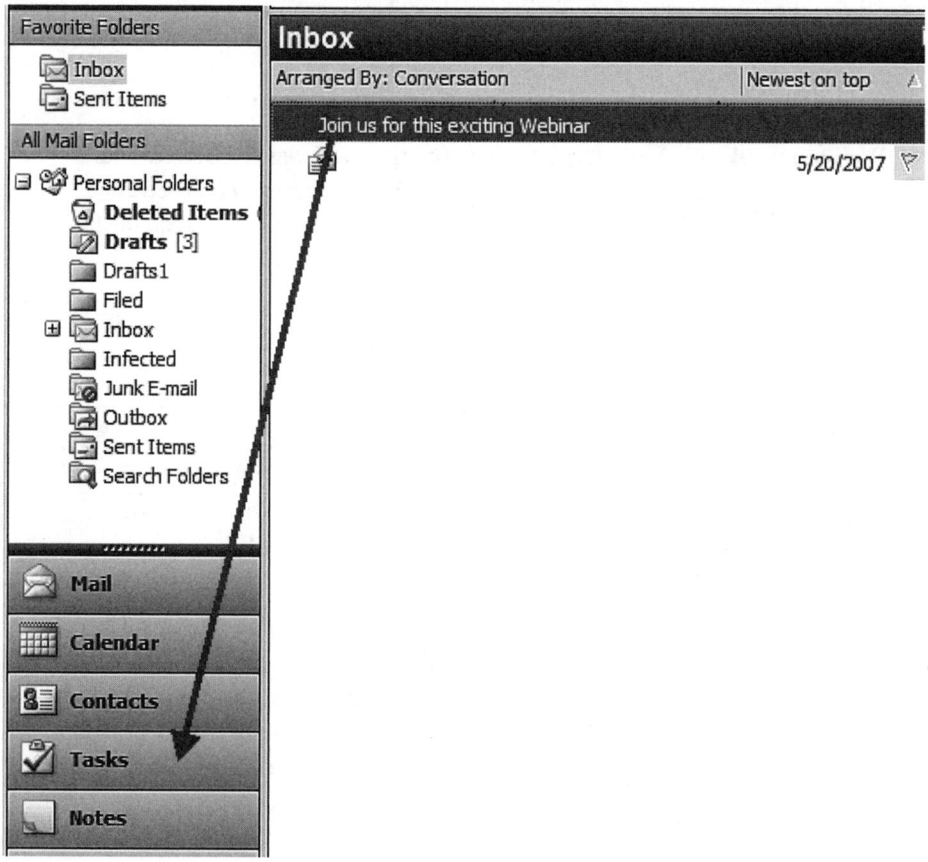

Figure 4.10. E-mail Text Displayed in Note Section of Task

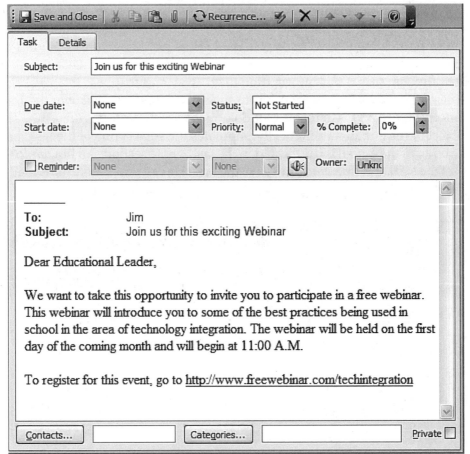

A Complete Contacts List

Contacts in Microsoft Outlook is the substitute for the paper address book you find yourself rewriting every couple of years. Figure 4.11 shows the elements at one's command for any contact. In addition to the fields for a host of information, Microsoft Outlook provides a large section for notes. The information you might include in this note section includes the following:

◆ Directions on how to get to that person's house or business

◆ Clothing sizes for relatives

◆ Names of your friends' children and their birthdays

◆ Your account number with a business

Figure 4.11. New Contact Record

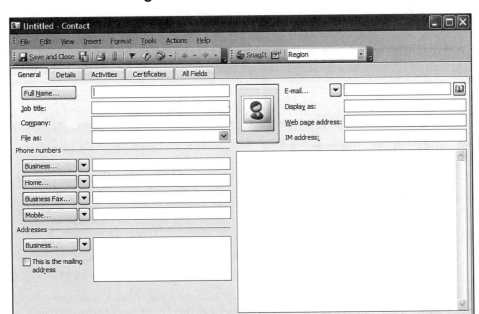

A Wealth of Reference Material

The Notes section of Microsoft Outlook is a place where you can store reference information. Here are some examples of the information which could be keep in Microsoft Outlook Notes:

◆ Numbers: One note can hold all the passwords for various web sites, the school system's federal tax identification number, the administrative code for the Xerox machine, and the burglar alarm code, just to name a few. It is amazing how many numbers we are expected to be able to produce. This one note can hold all of them.

◆ Checklists: We all have certain activities made up of a number of steps. A set of checklists keeps us from *reinventing the wheel* countless times.

◆ Documentation from calls and conferences: At times, the notes taken while on the phone are valuable because of the content. Other times we simply need to document what was said and agreed on in case disagreements arise later. The drag and drop feature is valuable here. If a task on the list is "Call Mrs. Jones," during the call use the note section of that task to document important points from the call. If those notes are of lasting value and must be retained notes indefinitely, drag the task over the Notes button. Microsoft Outlook automatically creates a new note. The program even date- and time-stamps the note.

◆ Descriptions of each of the workshops one conducts: If you conduct workshops or seminars, a brief description of each is a helpful piece of information to have at hand.

◆ Devotionals, inspirational messages, and quotes: As school leaders, we are often called on to offer a devotional or inspirational message or simply to *say a few words* before a meeting or meal. Usually, these requests come on the spur of the moment. Having a few of these gems tucked neatly away in your signature tool comes in handy.

◆ Data: What are some significant facts and figures from the latest standardized test? What data could you site related to the progress of your school? When addressing parent groups or talking to the local news reporter, having some facts and figures handy pays big dividends.

◆ Staff list: You will need a staff *check-off* list countless times during the year.

◆ Common documents, legislation, and policies: Would you like to have a copy of the Declaration of Independence at hand? Do you find yourself referring to a particular Board of Education policy or state statute often? Each of these is a candidate for a note in Microsoft Outlook.

The *Mother Ship* and the Satellite

Most of this discussion has been a methodology for using Microsoft Outlook at your desk, and for good reason. A command of Microsoft Outlook is a precursor for establishing a complete system on the handheld device. Operating a keyboard with 10 fingers is far quicker and easier than entering information with two thumbs. *Heavy-duty entry* is done in Microsoft Outlook. It is helpful to think of the desktop computer as the *mother ship* and the handheld as a satellite.

Interestingly enough, as soon as desktop computers became commonplace, *Personal Information Manager* software began to appear. The capabilities of those programs were similar to those of Microsoft Outlook. However, when you got up from your computer, you were also getting up from your calendar, to-do list, and address book. The advent of the Palm Pilot changed all of that. Synchronizing the handheld device with the desktop software allows you to walk away from the computer with all the information in your pocket. Access to all that valuable data is effortless, regardless of location. This 1-minute ritual is the first thing to do on arrival at work and the last thing to do before going home in the evening.

Any handheld device comes with an instruction manual that explains the function of each button and the list of choices of each menu. Numerous books are devoted to operating instructions for specific devices. By intention, this chapter makes no attempt to duplicate what is already available through those venues. However, most publications neglect any type of comprehensive system for organizing information and ensuring that information appears at the right time and in the most helpful format. This chapter, along with the upcoming chapter on project management, provides such a system.

Paper or digital? The decision for your signature tool rests as much with personal preference as anything else. You may have already made a decision. Perhaps that decision will be made as you work through the remainder of this book. That decision may even change over time as the complexity of your life changes.

Next Steps

- Reread Jim's typical day. How do you presently handle each of the scenarios described? What are the strengths and/or shortcomings of the system you presently use in terms of how you would handle each scenario?

- Schedule a trip to an office supply store or cellular phone provider and experiment with several of the handheld tools.

- Experiment with Microsoft Outlook. You could do so on your own computer or one in a computer lab. You might try duplicating some of the examples you have seen in this chapter.

- For the next several days, pay special attention to the amount of information that comes to you digitally. How much of it are you printing? Of that, how much is useful only for a short time and then discarded? How much is stored long term? How and where is it stored?

If your decision is to organize digitally, read the Appendix carefully and set up Microsoft Outlook in the manner outlined there. Realize that all things improve through practice. You will make mistakes as you begin working with both Microsoft Outlook and your digital signature tool. You will fumble. The investment of a little time and patience pays big dividends in the long run.

5

Think It Through Once: Handling Repeating Tasks

Making the simple complicated is commonplace; making the complicated simple, awesomely simple, that's creativity.

Charles Mingus

Education is a Cyclic Business

The start of each new school year brings plans for the months ahead. Some plans involve new projects and new ideas we will be trying. Other plans involve re-thinking some of the same thoughts covered last year. What tasks do we need to perform to be *ready* when students walk through the door? What materials will we need? What instructions need to be given to teachers? What orientation activities will we have for new students?

As we think through the year, what field trips or other special projects will be undertaken? What plans need to be made? Do we need to reserve buses? What information will we prepare and send to parents? What purchase orders will be needed?

The old saying "the devil is in the details" is certainly true in education. Let one of the myriad of details slip through the cracks and you are faced with a group of students ready for the field trip and no bus! Not only that, but there are no sack lunches prepared for the students because you forgot to speak to the lunchroom manager about preparing them. The check you must present at your destination almost didn't get written because you forgot to request it until yesterday afternoon.

The good news for those of us in the business of education is that many of the same *devils* return every year and at the same time. The first time a big project such as starting a school year or planning the trip to Washington is undertaken, little to-dos occur to you at the most unlikely of moments—in the middle of a meeting, during lunch, or while pushing the shopping cart down the aisle of the grocery store. When they occur, the habit of capturing them with the signature tool keeps a good idea or essential detail from disappearing.

There is even better news. Once a project has been handled once, you should never have to rethink any of those details. Never again will you sit with a blank legal pad 3 weeks before the start of school trying to pull a list out of your head of what must be done. Never again will you rethink all the details that went into the big *spring production*. The truth of the matter is all the details to handle *this* year are the same ones handled *last* year. You only need a system to keep track of them.

This chapter provides a system to identify and capture all the repeating tasks that come your way. Without such a plan, you are in for a frustrating experience as you *reinvent the wheel* year after year.

Setting Up a Repeating Task System

To make life much easier, establish a system to handle all the details that recur each year, month, week, or even each day. The first step in establishing this tool is to become very good at recognizing tasks that will recur as soon as they appear. Consider these two items:

1. Call Mrs. Smith
2. Order laminating film

Each represents a simple phone call. Each can be handled in just a few minutes. Each could probably be delegated. However, the two are vastly different. Once the call to Mrs. Smith is completed, the task is checked off and nothing more must be done. Conversely, ordering laminating film for the coming school year is a task that happens every summer. Every elementary school principal knows that approaching the start of the school year without laminating film would be a huge problem!

Getting very good at recognizing repeating tasks when they first present themselves is crucial in keeping things from falling through the cracks. When you find yourself writing a task that repeats at regular intervals, take the time to do something about it. A wise leader is sure to take time to recognize and organize repeating tasks. This practice saves time and effort when those tasks return a week, a month, or a year later. How can this organization occur? Here are three alternatives.

Repeating Tasks on Index Cards

Used in conjunction with tickler files, index cards offer a low-tech method for ensuring repeating tasks are completed according to schedule without giving them another thought. Each time you identify a repeating task, take an index card and write the task in the middle of the card. Toward the bottom of the card, write instructions on how the card should be refiled once the task has been completed.

As a beginning principal, the thought may occur to you during the summer to review the schedule for the custodians. You would be inclined to jot that task on your list and check it off after completion. The problem with this approach is there is no trigger to remind you about this task a year later. Instead, you must realize that updating this schedule is something that occurs not one time, but instead returns every summer. Using the index card system, pull a blank card and notate on it something like what you see in Figure 5.1.

Figure 5.1. Using Index Cards for Repeating Tasks

Update custodial schedule
Re-file for June 10 of next year

Once the instructions are written on the card, you never again have to *remember* to update the custodial schedule. Once you update the schedule, simply drop the card in the tickler file for June and forget about it. Next June, the card reappears. Perform the task again and refile the card.

Once a school leader truly identifies all the routine tasks performed during the course of the year, the number may well run up to several hundred. With the index card system, these routine tasks pop up at just the right time. An even more efficient system is to set up an index card and tickler file system with an administrative assistant and delegate many of the routine tasks. The important point is that the system does the remembering, and you are now free to move on to more creative thought.

Repeating Task List

An advantage of the index card is its simplicity. The disadvantage is the inability to see all the repeating tasks at once. One cannot see a total picture of just how many of them exist, how heavy or light any particular time of the year may be, or which tasks must be handled personally versus which can be delegated.

A second option exists for those using a paper signature tool: Put the repeating tasks together on one chronological list. To establish this list, the following procedure may prove helpful:

◆ Every time a task is added in your signature tool, pay special attention to whether it will be performed at routine intervals. Put a *red star* beside any such task.

◆ Perform the task and check it off. The number of red stars naturally increases over the course of the next few months.

◆ During the winter holidays, compile a Repeating Task List. Collect the pages from your signature tool for the last several months. Use them to create a new word processing document entitled, "Repeating Tasks List."

◆ Carefully examine all the past pages from the signature tool looking for red stars. Add each starred item to your list. Group the tasks chronologically by month.

◆ During the summer, compile the same type of list with the red star items collected between the winter break and present. Print the list, put a staple in one corner, and the entire year's inventory of repeating tasks is at your fingertips.

◆ Keep the Repeating Task List in your tickler file. Each time it pops up, perform the task and then refile the entire list for next date it is needed.

The Repeating Task List is an idea that works regardless of a person's particular position. As one moves from the classroom to a building-level administrative position, or the central office, the nature of the tasks on the list changes. However, the basic idea remains the same.

The Repeating Task List is ideal for handling responsibilities that arise no more frequently than once per month. For weekly or daily repeating tasks, use the index cards process.

Figure 5.2 shows a few sample tasks from a principal's repeating list for July. The complete list for July extended for more than two single-spaced pages. None were particularly difficult to perform, yet even the simplest one allowed to slip through the cracks would have caused this principal problems later. Every administrator has repeating tasks that are unique to the specific school or situation. The school leader must develop the ability to recognize a repeating task immediately and be able to put it in a system that can do the remembering.

Figure 5.2. Sample Repeating Task List

- Update forms for this month from monthly tickler on computer
- Compile order for school store
- Reset attendance flags to No
- Compose press release regarding registration
- Write press release on new course offerings
- Plan holiday gifts for teachers (Halloween, Christmas, Valentine's Day)
- Back up computer
- Schedule dates of assembly programs for coming year
- Schedule dates for school pictures (fall, spring, Santa)
- Arrange for fire extinguishers to be checked and serviced
- Prepare list of needed office supplies
- Examine playground equipment for needed repairs

Repeating Tasks in Microsoft Outlook

Repeating tasks are a breeze for those who organize digitally. Each time a repeating task arises, click the Recurrence button, and define how often the task should show up on the list. Figure 5.3 shows where repeating patterns would be established on Microsoft Outlook. Handheld devices have a similar option.

Figure 5.3. Repeating Task in Outlook

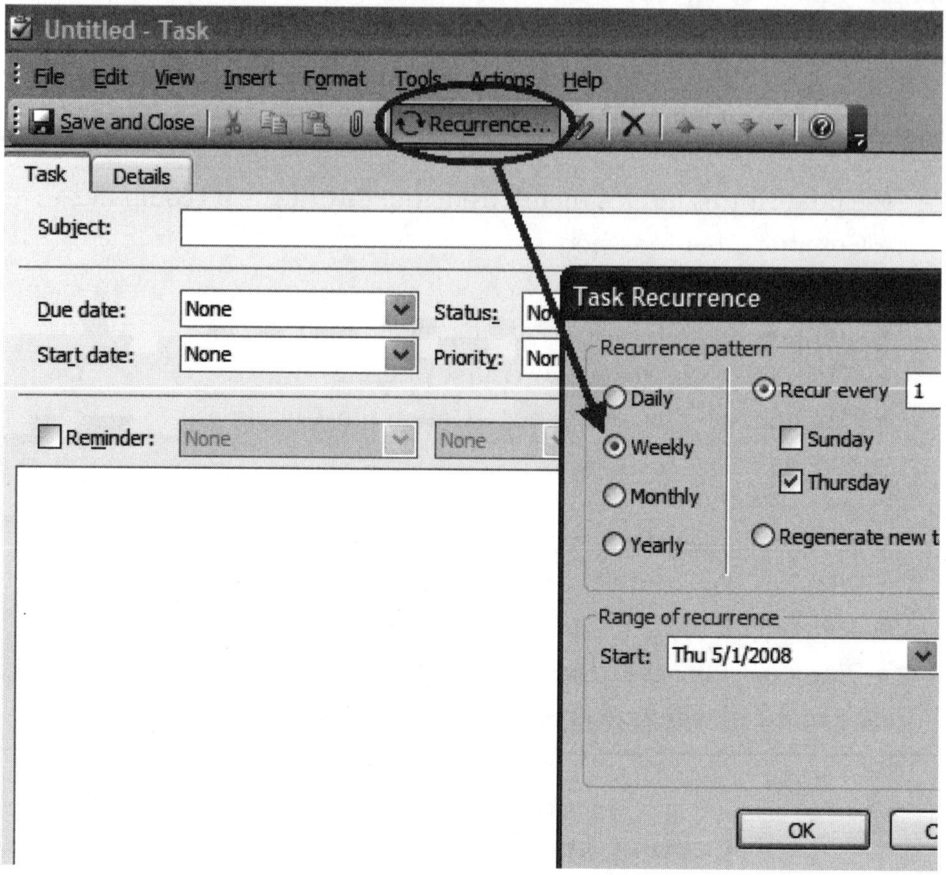

Keeping Your Sanity with Repeating Tasks

Visit the office of any school leader, and you are likely to see a shelf or more of manuals, each filled with tasks to be performed. A principal may be responsible for following procedures and policies from each of the following notebooks, just to name a few:

 ◆ Teacher Evaluation Manual: This manual, perhaps more than 4 inches thick, is laden with timelines and procedural land mines.

 ◆ Crisis Plan: Nobody doubts the importance of keeping students safe. However, a thick manual is not easily accessible and practical in a real crisis and does not necessarily ensure a safe school.

 ◆ State Law: One volume of the state code covers the laws governing education. Many procedures must be carried out annually because of requirements found in that book.

- ◆ Board of Education Policy: Imbedded are tasks that must be performed at various points in the year. Trying to commit each of them to memory and hoping one thinks to perform them at the right time is asking for trouble.
- ◆ Course of Study: With all the manuals on the shelf, let us not forget the reason schools exist is to teach students. The course of study for each discipline outlines content, requirements for graduation, and time requirements.

Each thick manual is written in isolation. No one ties them together for the principal. No one combs through the collection and hands the principal a comprehensive list of what must be done in August to satisfy the requirements of all the various sources. No one puts it all together in one big *ball of wax*. That job is for the principal. A similar scenario exists for the superintendent, curriculum director, assistant principal, department head, or anyone else who has assumed a leadership role in the school system.

The good news is that there is a way to preserve some sanity: the Repeating Task System. While reading through any one of those manuals, routine tasks leap off the page. At that point put them in the system. Jot them on index cards for the tickler files, add them to the repeating list, or enter them as repeating tasks in Microsoft Outlook. Now forget about them and trust your system to bring each one to your attention at the right time. Whether the task involves ordering laminating film, arranging for the inspection of fire extinguishers, conducting the various parts of the teacher evaluation, or scheduling fire drills at the prescribed interval, your Repeating Task System is the glue or the whole ball of wax that puts all the tasks in one place and makes them *get in line*.

Expanding the Repeating Task List Throughout the School

The school leader has the opportunity to expand the Repeating Task List throughout the organization. When a principal maintains a repeating list, personally performed tasks *will* be accomplished. The principal is responsible for far more, however. A large part of the principalship consists of getting work done through other people. The principal cannot and should not handle every detail of operating a school. This leader should, however, have a good understanding of what should be happening throughout the school at any point in the year. The principal should know what projects the counselor will undertake in September, what tasks the child nutrition manager will perform prior to the start of school, and how the librarian is structuring the year.

The entire staff may assist the principal in a concerted effort to identify all the repeating tasks throughout the building and ensure that someone is responsible for each. Place all the tasks on a spreadsheet. Label the columns with the name of the task, the person responsible, and the due date for each task.

Using a spreadsheet to structure this list allows the list to be sorted in a variety of ways. Sorting the list by *Person Responsible* allows a list to be printed for each person. Chronologically sorting the list allows the principal to view everything that should be witnessed happening in the school.

The time spent creating this list is recouped many times over in the time saved as well as in the stress relieved. With all the tasks captured on the Repeating Task List, principals need not worry about what may be slipping through the cracks. There is no need to reinvent the wheel each time a project is repeated. Let the list handle the details and free the principal to focus on more creative activities.

Next Steps

- ◆ Decide how to structure your repeating tasks. Will you use index cards dropped in tickler files, a list composed and saved on the computer, or repeating tasks on a digital tool?

- ◆ Schedule a block of time to think through the projects you handle each year. List all the tasks associated with each one. Review the list several times to see if additional tasks come to mind.

- ◆ Decide if the idea of the Repeating Task List is something you would like to expand throughout the organization. Consider asking the assistant principal, counselors, librarian, and department heads to construct a repeating task list for their positions. Do the same with the child nutrition manager and head custodian. Consider the same procedure for each central office administrator. Expand the idea to include the school administrative assistant and teachers who sponsor particular activities.

6

Handling
Multiple Projects

The secret of getting ahead is getting started. The secret of
getting started is breaking your complex and overwhelming
tasks into small manageable tasks and then starting on the
first one.

Mark Twain

Our proudest accomplishments and our more disheartening frustrations
are often associated with goals we have set and ambitious projects we have
undertaken. They were not accomplished with one simple act. Instead, over a
period of time they were mapped, adjusted along the way, and followed
through; problems were solved as glitches arose. The end result was a *job well
done*.

Conversely, we all can name a few endeavors we would like to forget.
The job kept bogging down. We were never quite sure what had been done
and what needed to be done next. The whole thing was a big, ugly fog that
finally died a natural death to which we exclaimed, "Good riddance!"

What Makes Projects Different?

Projects are entirely different from other tasks on the list. Checking off a single task does not complete a project or realize a goal. We achieve goals and handle projects through *multiple steps*. Sometimes, we can list every step in the project from beginning to end. With others the steps unfold as we work. To compound the problem, school leaders are generally handling multiple projects at any one time. How in the world can we keep it all straight?

The following example illustrates how complex even a relatively simple project can become. Imagine a principal of an older school notices one warm spring day that the paint is peeling from the wooden ceilings in two classrooms. The goal would obviously be to get those ceilings scraped and painted. The principal knows the first step toward accomplishing the goal is clear. It involves a simple phone call the head of the school system's maintenance department to report the problem. What about the second step? That answer is not so clear.

The call might very well elicit a response that the maintenance department had the time, manpower, and paint on hand. A promise is made that a crew would take care of the job that very afternoon. Conversely, the principal could be told that funds were tight and that the superintendent would need to be consulted about the need. A third scenario might be an upfront assurance the maintenance budget was dry, and the principal should handle the job with school funds. In this case, like many others, the first step toward achieving the goal of repainted ceilings was clear: talking to the head of the maintenance department. The outcome of that one conversation could lead to any of three entirely different second steps. Each response would send the project in a different direction, and that is after only one step! Imagine how many different twists and turns could take place between the day the peeling paint was noticed and the day the ceilings are painted.

Projects often work just that way. Keep in mind this is but one project. At the same time, the principal may be tracking as many as 50 of them ranging in various degrees of complexity and various degrees of completion.

Keeping projects on track involves some specific strategies, which are described throughout this chapter:

- ◆ Define the goal
- ◆ Break the project into small steps
- ◆ Feed projects into the task list
- ◆ Keep related notes with the project
- ◆ Stick with a project as long as you can
- ◆ Put a *bookmark* in the project

- Handle supporting material
- Link the tickler files to the task list

Define the Goal

Handling a project begins with defining the goal. What will the project look like when complete? How will you know when you have achieved your goal? Taking the time to state your goals clearly saves a great deal of time implementing them. Figure 6.1 is an example of projects the school leader may be addressing.

Figure 6.1. Example of Defined Goals

Write a goal as a statement written in the past tense. Word it as if it has already been achieved. Place a noun toward the beginning of the statement. Each statement is either *true* or *false*. Once that statement is true, the project can be checked off as done. As long as the statement is false, more work is ahead.

Your signature tool is the place to record the goal. Exactly where should it be recorded? The answer depends on the tool. Using a paper system, include blank pages in the back of the planner. Devote anywhere from a quarter of a page to the entire front and back of a page depending on the complexity of the project. Label the name of the project at the top of the page and number it. Write the goal at the top of the page. In the space available, write all the steps that occur to you as well as any related information that comes your way. Figure 6.2 gives an example of a project planning page.

Figure 6.2. Project Planning Page

Calendar for new school year has been adopted.

- ◆ Establish initial meeting.
- ◆ Send out invitations for initial meeting.
- ◆ Establish agenda for initial meeting.
- ◆ Publicize two calendars for votes.
- ◆ Establish meeting to tally votes.
- ◆ Establish dates for kindergarten registration, reporting period dates, and report cards dates.
- ◆ Make recommendation to superintendent.
- ◆ Publicize new calendars to schools.

Topics to discuss:

- ◆ Spring break after testing?
- ◆ Concentrate professional development days at beginning of year or space throughout the year?
- ◆ Fall break or not?
- ◆ Equal days first and second semesters?

If the signature tool is digital, enter the goal in the task list. Notice that each goal in Figure 6.1 begins with a + sign. That symbol sets a goal apart from the single tasks on the list. The + sign sitting at the beginning of the line serves as an alert that an important element is missing. That omission is discussed in the next section.

Break the Project Into Small Steps

With some projects it is possible to define all the steps from the beginning to end. With others, it may be possible to define only the next step. As with the example of painting the classroom ceilings, the principal could only define the first step.

For those who use a paper system, list on the project planning page all the steps you know, just as shown in Figure 6.2. For those using a digital tool, the place to list this information is in a note attached to the task. Figure 6.3 shows a sample project planned on Microsoft Outlook. Figure 6.4 provides an example on a handheld device.

Figure 6.3. Project Planning in Microsoft Outlook

```
 ┌──────────────────────────────────────────────────────────────────────────┐
 │  💾 Save and Close  │ ✂ 📋 📋 📎  🔄 Recurrence...  🗲 │ ✕ │ ▲ ▾ ▾ │ ⓪     │
 ├──────────────────────────────────────────────────────────────────────────┤
 │  Task   Details                                                            │
 │                                                                            │
 │   Subject:      +Evaluations have been completed                           │
 │   ───────────────────────────────────────────────────────────────────     │
 │                                                                            │
 │   Due date:    None              ▾   Status:   Not Started            ▾    │
 │   Start date:  None              ▾   Priority: Normal ▾  % Complete: 0% ▴▾ │
 │                                                                            │
 │   ☐ Reminder:  None          ▾   None       ▾  🔊  Owner:  Unknown        │
 │  ────────────────────────────────────────────────────────────────────     │
 │   Determine who is going through full evaluation                           │
 │   Copy correct number of PEPE spreadsheets into Current Evaluations folder │
 │   Prepare correct number of support person evaluation forms                │
 │   Schedule orientation for those going through full evaluation             │
 │   Set deadline for Professional Development Plan to be submitted for approval (Fall)│
 │   Set date for PDP to be submitted for evaluation (Spring)                 │
 │   Set deadline for structured interview                                    │
 │   Schedule 1st round of observations                                       │
 │   Schedule 2nd round of observations                                       │
 │   Schedule 3rd round of observations                                       │
 │   Complete Supervisor's Review Form                                        │
 │   Score PDPs                                                               │
 │   Complete Evaluation Summary Report                                       │
 │   Schedule evaluation conferences                                          │
 └──────────────────────────────────────────────────────────────────────────┘
```

Figure 6.4. Project Planning on a Handheld

```
 ┌────────────────────────────────┐
 │       Grading Period End        │
 ├────────────────────────────────┤
 │ Allow grade posting             │
 │ Remind teachers to post grades  │
 │ Run check to see who has not posted│
 │ grades                          │
 │ Run Marking Period Report       │
 │ Disallow grade posting          │
 │ Reconcile grades (Utilities, Grading,│
 │ Reconcile Grades)               │
 │ Run report cards                │
 │ Run Honor Rolls                 │
 │ Send Honor Rolls to media       │
 │                                 │
 │  ( Done )  ( Delete... )        │
 └────────────────────────────────┘
```

Feed Projects Into the Task List

Paper Signature Tool

With a paper-based signature tool, you must somehow link the project planning sheet in the back of the planner to the task list from which you are working. To do this take the first step from one of the projects and enter it into the task list. Beside the task, list the project number in parentheses. This action creates a link between the task in the list and the goal. In Figure 6.5 the notation (P1) denotes this task is from Project #1.

Figure 6.5. Task Linked Backed to Its Project

Harry—Send me copy of your proposed calendar (P1).

When the task is completed, that notation (P1) becomes important. Before checking the task off as done, go to the back of the planner and pick up the next task listed for that project. Every time one step in the project is completed, the next step must be added to the task list. Otherwise, the project falls through the cracks.

Digital Signature Tool

If the signature tool is digital, feeding projects into the task list is even easier. Notice that Figure 6.1 listed a series of goals. In each case the line began with a + sign and to the right was the goal. For each goal take the next step toward achieving that goal and place it to the left of the + sign. Figure 6.6 shows tasks and goals together. Working through the task list, the user can see *what* to do (the task) as well as *why* it is being done (the goal).

Figure 6.6. Tasks and Goals Together

When you complete a task, do not click the check box. Instead, replace the task just completed with the next step toward completing the project or achieving the goal. Figure 6.7 shows a project in Microsoft Outlook regarding hiring a teacher. The first task is "Talk to superintendent regarding resignation and filling position." When this task is completed, cut the task "Position posted" from the note section and paste it right over the task just completed.

Figure 6.7. Replacing One Task With the Next One

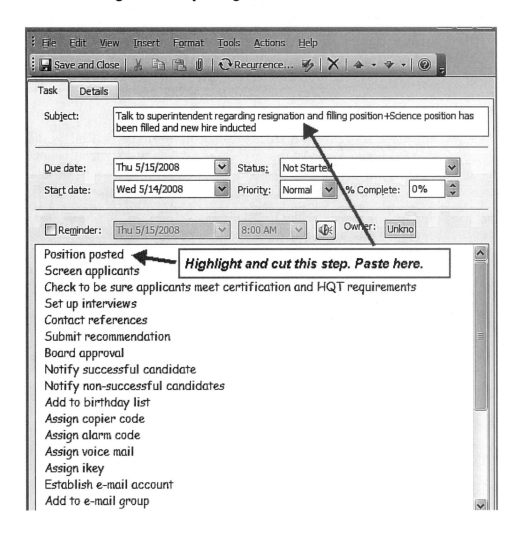

Keep Related Notes With the Project

During the life of any project, information is generated about it. If the goal is to establish a new computer lab, for example, at some point a list of various models and prices along with contact information for vendors is developed. Phone calls are probably made and notes taken during those calls. There may be information from e-mails or web pages. If all the information related to a project is kept together, finding that information becomes easy.

Paper Signature Tool

If you are using a paper tool, the project planning page is the place to keep notes from phone calls and any other information related to the project. Figure 6.2, viewed earlier in this chapter, provides an illustration.

Digital Signature Tool

If you are using a digital signature tool, all information related to the project goes in the note section of the task. Figure 6.8 shows a goal, the next step toward achieving it, a list of steps to follow, notes from a phone call, and Internet links to related information. When synchronized with the handheld, the school leader literally has all this information in the palm of the hand.

Figure 6.8. Information in Note Section of Task

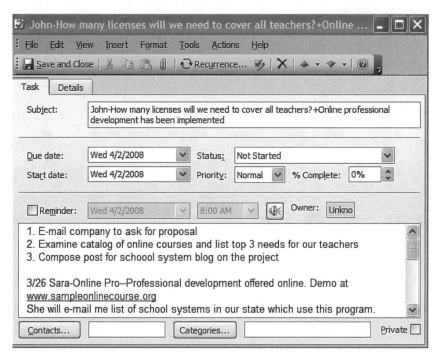

Stick With a Project as Long as You Can

One look at the task list reveals multiple projects represented. Should you perform the next step for Project 1, move to the next step for Project 2, and then handle the next step for Project 3? Should you stay with one project instead?

More is accomplished in the long run by sticking with one project as long as possible. One always experiences some *start-up* time when transitioning to a project, as well as gathering materials and getting mentally reacquainted with the project. More jumping back and forth from one project to the next means more time spent with these transition activities.

Suppose you wanted to work on hiring the science teacher, a scenario examined earlier. Figure 6.9 lists the steps. Having already spoken with the superintendent about being able to post and fill this position, the next step on the list is to be sure the vacancy notice for the position is posted. Once this step is complete, you may easily handle the next several steps in one single block of time.

Figure 6.9. Working Through a Single Project

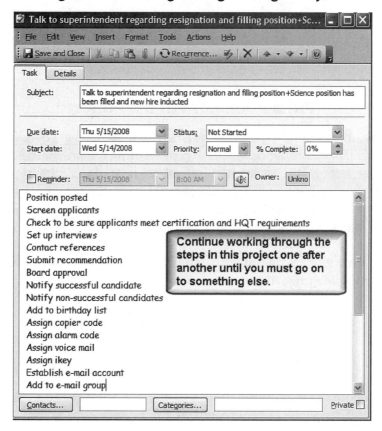

Looking at the task list, you could screen applicants and select those whose qualifications seem appealing. Continuing with the same project, you could focus specifically on whether or not each of the prospects meets Highly Qualified Teacher status. The administrative assistant could then telephone candidates to set up interviews. This method is the most efficient for handling projects. Stick with one project as long as possible, and simply move from one step to the next.

At some point you cease working on that project. Any number of reasons could account for needing to move on to something else:

- ◆ You have an appointment and need to move on to it.
- ◆ You have other urgent matters that need your attention and cannot afford to spend any more time on this project at this time.
- ◆ You are getting tired and need a break from the project.
- ◆ You need information that you do not have at hand to continue the project.
- ◆ You see that the next step in the project is to contact another person, and that person is unavailable.
- ◆ You are interrupted by an emergency.

The list could go on. Whatever the reason for putting the project aside, you need a *bookmark*.

Put a *Bookmark* in the Project

At one time or another, each of us has read a book from cover to cover in one sitting. This experience is the exception rather than the rule. For one reason or another, the book must be put aside to do something else. Just before closing the book, we *insert a bookmark*. This little tool indicates exactly *where to begin* the next time we resume reading up the book. The same type of reminder is needed when working on our projects. We may work through step after step of a project. Just before we put the project aside, we must decide where to start with this project next time. That task must go on our list before leaving the project.

Handle Supporting Material

Managing a project includes organizing and quickly accessing the supporting material. For example, if the project is to write a grant, you should have the Request for Proposal, data others have supplied to you, letters of support, and pages of notes created. If the project is to set up a wireless computer network at home, you may have several articles clipped from magazines. If the project is to revise your school's writing program, you likely collected sample plans from other schools, articles from journals, and notes taken from workshops. Where do you keep all of this *stuff*? How do you link these items back to the project in your signature tool? The answer is to use the tickler files.

First, here is how *not* use the tickler files:

- ◆ *Do not* select a date to work on the grant and put the papers related to it in the folder for that date.
- ◆ *Do not* pick a date to work on the wireless network and file the supporting material for that date.
- ◆ *Do not* pick a date to work on the writing program and file the supporting material for that date.

At first glance, you may wonder what is wrong with such an approach. The problem is that a group of papers does not tell you *what* to do. At best, a collection of papers related to the grant serve as a reminder to do *something* about that grant. Your task list, and project planning sheet if planning with paper, is where you define exactly what to do next on the project and what steps follow. The supporting material does not drive the action. Instead, this material simply must be accessible when you need it.

In Chapter 2 we labeled hanging files 1 to 31 to make items go away and then come back on specific dates. We will now give the first 26 of those files a letter designation (1A, 2B, 3C . . . 26Z) and learn how to use those letters.

Link the Tickler Files to the Task List

As soon as the grant proposal crosses the desk, follow these nine steps to get the paper off of the desk yet easily retrievable, the tasks defined on the list, and achieve a clear head:

1. Scan the proposal quickly to determine what it is and if you wish to apply. For the sake of this example, suppose the grant is called, "Reading for the Next Century."

2. Assuming you plan to apply, create a new task in Microsoft Outlook and label the subject line "+Reading for the Next Century Grant has been submitted."

3. In the note section, enter important information gleaned from a quick glance at the proposal. Such information includes the due date, the grant award amount, and a one-sentence description of the grant. Of course during the writing of the grant, you will think of many more tasks associated with the project. Valuable information will come

your way, such as the name of someone else who was successful in writing a proposal for this grant in the past. Enter all this information in the note section of this one task.

4. You have supporting material in paper form. Go back to the subject line and add in parentheses "(R)." As with anything else in this system, a set of parentheses means *look here for additional information*. The subject line now reads, "+Reading for the Next Century Grant has been submitted (R)."

5. Grab a blank manila file folder and label it "Reading for the Next Century Grant (R)."

6. Open the tickler file drawer and place the file folder in the 18R folder and close the drawer.

7. Return to Microsoft Outlook and ask the question, "What is the first step toward completing this project?"

8. Once you determine the first step, enter it to the left of the +.

9. Choose an appropriate start and due date and save the task.

Now go on to anything else. The first step in completing this project has been defined and is in the task list. If you think of ideas related to this project, go back to Microsoft Outlook, double-click on the project, and add the new ideas in the note section. If the paperwork associated with the project is needed, simply thinking about the name of the grant reveals where to go in the tickler files to find it. Figure 6.10 provides a screen shot of how the project will look.

Figure 6.10. Project Involving a Reading Grant

Task	Details

Subject: +Reading for the Next Century Grant has been submitted (R)

Due date:	Thu 7/10/2008 ▾	Status:	Not Started
Start date:	Sun 6/1/2008 ▾	Priority:	Normal ▾ % Complete: 0%

☑ Reminder: Thu 7/10/2008 ▾   8:00 AM ▾   🔊   Owner: |

Due August 1
$30,000
Purpose is to raise reading achivement among students from high-poverty background

Previous winners–Jefferson Elementary (www.jeffelem.org); Coker School www.cokerschool.com)

The same concept is used for any papers that require action, yet have no associated date. This next example uses a paper planner as the signature tool. Suppose you are reading a magazine article about setting up a wireless network at home and contemplate doing the same thing. Follow these six steps:

1. Clip the article.
2. Take 2 seconds to determine what key word would be associated with this article. Perhaps the first thought is *wireless.*
3. Flip to the back of the planner to a blank page and write on the top line, "Wireless network has been set up at home. (W)"
4. On the article, write "(W)" in the upper right hand corner.
5. Open the tickler file drawer and put the article in the 23W file.
6. Decide what the first step toward completing this project is going to be. Perhaps you are going to ask a colleague (John in this example) for his recommendations. In the planner, this task would look like Figure 6.11.

Figure 6.11. Wireless Home Network Project

Wireless network has been set up at home (W).

1. John: What are your recommendations?
2. Google: Wireless network purchasing.
3. Call Computer World: 555–8181. Ask about upcoming sales.

Whether the subject is the reading grant, the wireless network, or any project, the signature tool manages the flow of the project. If supporting material exists, the use of parentheses at the end of the task line points to that supporting material. If someone wants to see the paperwork on the "Reading for the Next Century Grant," think in terms of the key word *reading* and immediately pull the material from the R folder.

It's Morning at the Office

When I arrive at the office, opening Microsoft Outlook and pulling the tickler file for the day are the first two orders of business. In the tickler folder, I see two types of items:

1. Items related to that *date.* At some point I decided these papers needed to come back to my attention on this particular day, such as the birthday card that needs to go in the mail today, the agenda for to-day's Board of Education meeting, or the tickets to tonight's concert. These papers are removed from the tickler file and handled.

2. Items related to that *letter.* Examples include the manila file with the grant materials or the wireless network article. I leave these items in the folder and place this file at the back of the rack, where it resurfaces a month from now.

How do I quickly tell which items are date specific and which constitute supporting material for items on the task list? If an item is supporting material, in the upper right corner, I see a *letter in parentheses.* The wireless network article has a "(W)" in the upper right corner. In my signature tool, the project ends with a "(W)," pointing me to the supporting material.

Building a Reputation for *Staying on Top of Things*

You can stay on top of multiple projects. At times, you may feel like a juggler. In a way your role in handling multiple projects and the role of a juggler are much the same. A juggler keeps a number of balls in the air by *giving each one a little attention on a regular basis.* The juggler knows just how many objects are in the air, where each one is, when attention is needed, and how much attention is needed. We need to know exactly the same thing about each of our projects.

Certainly, none of us should take on more than we can handle well. For each of us, a limit exists. The reality of school leadership is that we have much on our plates. We need tools to help us stay on top of it all. This chapter gives you those tools. You cannot only handle multiple projects, but you can make it look easy.

Next Steps

◆ Schedule a time to make a list of the projects currently in progress or planned for the future. Do not try to fill in details at this point.

◆ Once you have identified all the projects, enter each one in your signature tool. If that tool is paper, devote anywhere from a fourth of a page to the front and back of a full page, depending on the complexity. If that tool is digital, create a new task for each, start the line with a +, and define your goal.

◆ Begin with the projects already in progress. List as many steps in the project as possible. For those using a digital signature tool, list the steps in the note section of each task.

◆ Pull together information about the projects that are on scraps of paper or you have been trying to remember. Enter all that information with its project.

◆ Identify the next step in each project and enter each in your task list.

◆ For projects you will not begin until sometime in the future, do not worry about identifying the first step in the project. For digital tools, the + with nothing to the left identifies that project as one not currently moving forward.

7

Reference Material: Short Term and Long Term

The average organization makes 19 copies of each document, spends $20 in labor to file each document, spends $120 in labor searching for each misfiled document, loses one out of every 20 documents, and spends 25 hours recreating each lost document.

PricewaterhouseCoopers

Discussions to this point have centered on *action* items. The systems outlined in this book prompt us to *doing*. All the notes and material in the tickler files are related to well-defined goals. This chapter examines a system for handling reference information. We do not know when or if we will need the information again. The important element is that if we need it, we can find it quickly.

A to Z Files

Somewhere between action items and true reference items is material to store for the short term. How often do you receive paperwork that you may never need again, yet you are not comfortable throwing it away? A flyer for a workshop comes in the mail. You are not interested in going; but just as it is thrown away, a teacher asks about the information for that very workshop.

Today's mail includes a letter from Mr. Smith. No action is required, and it is probably the only letter you will receive from Mr. Smith all year. Creating a file folder for one letter seems a waste. What do you do with this type of information? What sort of system can be devised to quickly file such information yet find it again with little trouble?

I devote one filing cabinet drawer to this type of material. The file drawer contains 26 hanging file folders labeled A to Z. The letter from Mr. Smith goes in the *back* of the S folder. The flyer for the Acme workshop goes in the back of the A folder. You may find there are a few people from whom numerous memos or other communication is received. Those people are assigned their own folders.

Why file to the *back* of the folder? A Stanford University study revealed that 87% of filed papers were never looked at again (Pollar, 2007). You do not anticipate ever needing any piece of paper put in the A to Z files again. This system holds onto them *just in case*. For this reason you need a filing system that takes no time to file. Putting the Smith letter in the back of the S file takes 2 seconds. Trying to keep the S file in alphabetical order, filing the letter between Sk and Sn, slows down the process.

For times when papers must be retrieved from the A to Z files, you will know which file to access. Now, think about *what time of year* the item arrived. Items from the first of the year are found toward the first of the folder. Anything that came toward the middle of the year is toward the middle of the folder. Within each file, therefore, papers are filed *chronologically* rather than *alphabetically*.

One repeating summertime task is to purge the set of A to Z files. By that time you have a solid idea of what can be thrown away and what is potentially of lasting value. Stack the entire set on the desk, open the A folder, and look at each piece of paper for roughly 1 second. In that 1 second, make a decision to either trash it or keep it forever. All the *trash* items go in one stack. All the *keep* items go face down in another stack. By the time you have finished the exercise, the keep pile is likely quite thin. Do not be surprised if the trash pile stands several feet tall! At that point I take one file folder, label it "Correspondence [fill in year]," place the "keep" pile in the folder, and file the folder in my reference system. As for the other pile, sensitive items are shredded, and then it all goes in a large garbage bag. The A to Z set is now empty and ready for a new school year.

File It the Way You Find It

Simplifying filing spells the difference between an office clear of clutter and one where piles of papers laying around are the rule. The A to Z files provide an example of chronological filing. New items go behind old items.

The school leader will see other examples where chronological filing presents a huge time saver. Disciplinary referrals provide one such example for the building-level administrator. Imagine a middle school assistant principal who is responsible for handling the disciplinary referrals. After seeing the student and entering the information in the school administrative software, the assistant principal would likely file the paperwork alphabetically. After all, alphabetical filing is a system that seems comfortable. As the year progresses and the numbers of referrals have increased, filing each form takes more time. As a result the tendency exists to put off the job of filing. Soon, a huge backlog of unfiled forms clutters the office.

The savvy assistant principal may later realize that whenever a student's disciplinary record needs to be accessed, it is always done on the *computer*. No one needs to actually examine the *paper* form. From that day forward, the assistant principal begins *chronologically* filing those forms. At the end of the day, every disciplinary form that comes in during the day is placed in the *back* of the stack. That which had been a constant headache became a 2-second per day piece of cake!

The beginning of school is a time when a variety papers are collected and then purged at the end of the year. Examples include the page of the student handbook where students and parents sign to indicate they have read the handbook. Imagine the school where those forms are filed in individual student folders. The same process is repeated with several other forms, such as one parents signed agreeing to pay for textbooks lost by their children. Homeroom teachers collect the form from their students. When all students have turned in a particular form, the teacher puts a rubber band around the stack and sends it to the office.

The office staff then spends considerable time taking the individual pieces of paper, organized by homeroom, and filing them in individual student folders. When the school year is over, the office staff spends several days purging those same forms from all the student folders.

Think how much time would be saved on both ends of the school year by filing those forms *the way they came in*—handbook acknowledgments in one folder, textbook agreements in one folder, and so forth. Throw them in the correct folder as teachers turn them in. Throw the folders away at the end of the year. The process could not get any easier!

Long-Term Reference Files

Most every school leader has some type of long-term reference files housed in metal filing cabinets. Each file is labeled by subject, and files are organized alphabetically according to their labels.

Of everything discussed in this book, a reference filing system is probably the most universally familiar. The main reason for spending time on this subject is the introduction it provides to Chapter 8: setting up a filing system on the computer. A filing system on the computer is best patterned after the paper system already in place.

For this reason, the basic message here is to examine your present filing system and do whatever cleanup work must be done. Here are a few basic principles for setting up and maintaining a long-term reference files:

- ♦ Use manila file folders instead of hanging files. They take up far less room. This advice may seem to contradict the use of hanging files for tickler files and A to Z files. In both of those areas, however, papers as well as entire manila folders are placed in them.

- ♦ Use a noun to begin the file name.

- ♦ Use broad category names.

- ♦ Use subheadings to break down the broader categories, such as Assessment—Graduation Exam; Assessment—Stanford; Assessment—Writing. This arrangement keeps all assessment scores together. Files labeled Graduation Exam, Stanford, and Writing would be spread out in various parts of the filing cabinet.

- ♦ Annually examine the contents of the files. Although the system is designed for documents of long-term value, at some point certain material outlives its usefulness.

- ♦ For files in which no additional material will be added and are rarely accessed, consider storing them in another area of the building.

After the Dance:
What to Do When a Project is Complete

After reading the Chapter 6, you have a system for staying on top of multiple projects and seeing them to their completion. When the project is done, what happens to the project planning sheet in your paper signature tool or the task in your digital tool? What happens to the file of supporting material?

Consider whether or not you need a *paper trail*. Perhaps this same project or a similar one will be undertaken in the future. Perhaps the notes from this project will be shared with someone else. Depending on the project, the requirement that records be maintained for a period of time is highly probable. If you see no reason to keep any of the material, put the supporting paperwork in the trash can. Use a paper shredder for anything that could be confidential. Remember, the Stanford study shows that 87% of what you file will never be looked at again. If you are not required to keep it, and you see no value in keeping it, get rid of it.

The same is true of the project planning sheet from your paper signature tool. If it has no value, throw it away or shred it. For those with a digital signature tool, simple check the task off as done.

If you save records from your project, spending just a little time with cleanup makes the difference between concise records that are self-explanatory years later and the burden of picking up a thick, barely decipherable folder. Go through the supporting folder item by item. Get rid of duplicate copies and cryptic notes. If your signature tool is paper, the project planning sheet can also go in this same folder. If digitally organizing you may wish to print the task containing all of your notes and put it in this folder as well. Although I am not a fan of printing digital reference material, the benefits of keeping everything in one place outweigh the downside of creating more paper.

When the paperwork is neatly organized, label a single file folder, and let the completed project join the reference files. If someone needs to review the project, the information in the folder can be found quickly. The Chapter 8 explores what happens if much or all the project information is in a digital format.

Next Steps

- Secure a set of 26 hanging file folders and label them A to Z.
- Clear a filing drawer and set up your A to Z file there.
- Examine your present long-term reference filing system. What needs to be thrown away? What files should be moved to another location?
- Examine the filing system for any needing reorganization.
- Examine the files for improvements needed in labeling.

8

Organizing Your Computer

I do not fear computers. I fear the lack of them.

Isaac Asimov

Our culture has trouble filing and finding paper after centuries of experience dealing with paper. We should not be surprised to find many school leaders totally lost when attempting to organize files on the computer. The problem that results is an inability to trust any type of digital filing or retrieval system.

Setting Up a Digital Filing System

In your classroom or office you probably have a metal filing cabinet. Take a moment to see if you could answer *true* for each statement as it relates to that metal filing cabinet:

- *I know where the box of file folders is kept.* You would have quite a time organizing a filing cabinet with no folders!
- *I know how to label (or relabel) a blank file folder.* Could you imagine simply using whatever labels already happened to be on the folders from a previous use?

- *I have set up a logical filing system.* If not, you would be randomly tossing files into any drawer of the filing cabinet. It would be doubtful anything could be found later.

- *I pay attention to where I file things.* If not, consider everything in the filing cabinet lost.

- *I can find what I have filed.* If any of the preceding statements are false, by this point retrieval poses problems.

- *I routinely file papers.* Those who let them stack up *on top* of the filing cabinet must sort through the entire pile.

- *I have copies of important papers.* Ideally, it would be nice to have copies of all of your important papers filed off-site. In practice, making copies of all important papers and storing them in another location is impractical.

The preceding statements range from trite to ridiculous. Each statement, however, has a counterpart in the digital world. By looking at the two side by side, we can begin to see the problem people have when it comes to organizing their computers.

Paper: I know where the box of file folders is kept.

Digital Counterpart: *I can make a new folder when I need to do so.* A workshop conducted for the clerical staff in a school system revealed not one single person in the group knew how to perform this skill. Their ability to organize files on their computers was as poor as what they would experience trying to organize a metal filing cabinet with no file folders.

Paper: I know how to label (or relabel) a blank file folder.

Digital Counterpart: *I know how to label or relabel a folder.* Without this small skill, you will never have folders that are descriptive of what is in them.

Paper: I have set up a logical filing system.

Digital Counterpart: *I have set up a logical filing system.* Just as the absence of a logical filing system with a metal filing cabinet makes finding anything a challenge, the same is true on the computer.

Paper: I pay attention to where I file things.

Digital Counterpart: *I pay attention to where I file things.* Many people allow the computer to save files wherever it wants. You must make the decisions.

Paper: I can find what I have filed.

Digital Counterpart: *I can find what I have saved.* Just as with paper, if problems exist with any of the preceding statements, problems will exist here as well.

Paper: I routinely file papers.

Digital Counterpart: *I routinely clear my desktop.* You probably know people whose entire computer desktop is covered with icons and even have icons sitting on top of other icons. You may even be one of these people. When you are looking at *everything,* it becomes hard to find *anything.*

Paper: I have copies of important papers.

Digital Counterpart: *I have a good backup routine and backup regularly.* The number of people who have no backup system is amazing. One hard drive failure is all that is required for years of data to be lost.

After reading this chapter, you will be able to answer *true* to every one of those statements as it pertains to your digital filing system.

The Desktop

The starting point is the desktop and making decisions about what can stay there. For some people, the answer is *everything*! The whole desktop is full of icons, with icons sitting on top of other icons.

Limit the icons on the desktop to the following:

- The My Documents folder
- Any program you use all day every day, such as Microsoft Word, Microsoft Outlook, or your school administrative software
- Fingertip Files, those few files that you use very regularly (clarified later in the chapter)
- Current Projects (explained later in the chapter)
- The Internet browser

My Documents

The My Documents folder is the heart of the system. Think of it as the filing cabinet where you store all the work you create. To begin organizing My Documents, look first at your paper filing system. In the last chapter, we discussed tidying up that system. Once you are pleased with the paper filing system, create a *comparable* system on the computer. For example, if a science teacher was handed a good lesson plan on photosynthesis, the teacher would need a place in the filing cabinet for it. If the same teacher was given a PowerPoint presentation on photosynthesis, the teacher should have a place in the digital filing system to put that PowerPoint presentation.

Having a model often serves as a good starting point. Figure 8.1 provides an example of the folders in a typical My Documents. Feel free to pattern your own system after this one. Alter it to fit your particular situation.

Figure 8.1. Sample My Documents Folder

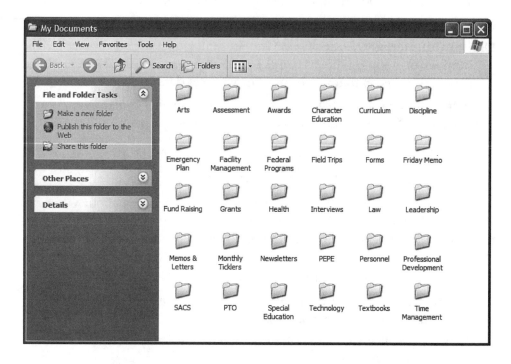

Creating, Naming, and Renaming a Folder

When creating a filing system, you need to know how to create new folders. The skill set for doing so is as follows:

- Right-click in the My Documents folder (or the folder where you want it to go).
- A menu appears.
- Choose *New*.
- When you highlight new, one of the options is *Folder* (Figure 8.2).
- You will see your new folder. The title is highlighted. Type the name for the folder (Figure 8.3).

If a folder needs to be renamed, right-click on the folder and choose *Rename*. The name is highlighted, and a new name for the file may be typed.

Figure 8.2. Creating a New Folder

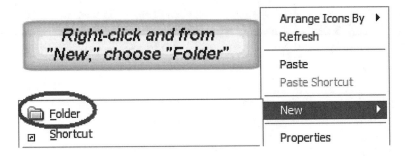

Figure 8.3. New Folder

Saving Documents Logically

How often do you dread saving documents for fear of never being able to find them again? Many people opt to print a hard copy in case they cannot find their work on the computer. When changes must be made, they wind up rekeying the entire document.

When saving a document, a dialog box appears and tells exactly where the file is going to be saved (Figure 8.4). By clicking *Save* the file is assigned the title shown in the File name line and saved in the spot shown in the "Save in" line. In this example the file is saved under the name *Very Important Document* and found in the My Documents folder.

Figure 8.4. Saving a Document

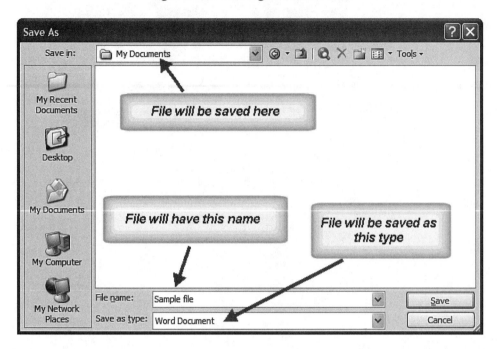

My Documents may be the desired location for the file. Then again, this location may not be the appropriate one. If the document is to be saved in one of the folders shown in the window, double-clicking on that folder puts that file name in the "Save in" line.

If you become puzzled, the easiest thing to do is just backup to the top level. Simply click on the folder with the *up* arrow until it won't go any further. *Desktop* appears in the window. Save the file. From there, drag the file into the appropriate file.

Memos & Letters

One of the folders in My Documents is called *Memos & Letters*. After composing a memo or letter, I never save a paper copy. Instead, I electronically file any type of correspondence in the folder called *Memos & Letters*. The key to finding these documents later is to develop a system for naming files.

My preference is to name files with the last name of the recipient followed by a hyphen, followed by several words that describe the subject matter of the document. Likewise, when receiving a document in digital fashion, I name the file with the sender's last name, a hyphen, and a few words descriptive of the subject matter. For example, if writing to someone asking for thoughts on playground equipment, there is no need to wonder weeks later when retrieving it whether the letter was named "Playground Letter," "Thoughts," or "New Playground." The document starts with the last name of the person, a hyphen, and a few words about the playground. Furthermore, it is in my Memos & Letters folder, which is located in the My Documents folder.

Monthly Ticklers

Another notable folder in My Documents is called *Monthly Ticklers*. Education is a cyclic business. We find ourselves engaged in the same projects at the same time each year. In many cases, a project involves updating the forms and other paperwork that goes with it. How nice would it be if all the routine paperwork we need to update in a given month was located in one place? The Monthly Ticklers folder is designed for just this function.

Inside the Monthly Ticklers folder are 12 folders labeled with the 12 months of the year. Each file contains the documents that must be updated during that month. For example, a principal's July folder (Figure 8.5) might contain the Faculty Handbook and Student Handbook. At the first of July, the principal opens the July folder. Seeing the Faculty Handbook and Student Handbook serve as reminders to update and print these two documents.

Figure 8.5. Monthly Tickler

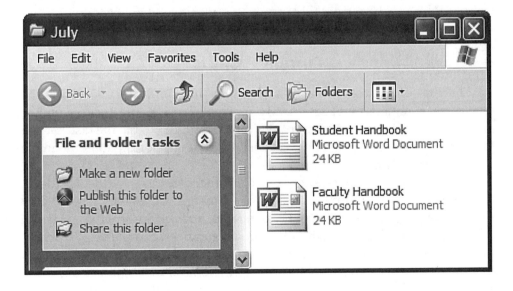

A secondary principal might have the subject selection forms in the March folder. At the beginning of March, seeing the contents of that folder serves as a reminder to update the forms with the date for the next school year, the addition of new courses, and the deletion of courses that will no longer be offered. Opening one of the monthly ticklers serves as the trigger to examine, update, and print each item in there.

Fingertip Files

Most people will find that 5% of their files account for 95% of the use. Having those files where they are easy to access is a time saver that pays daily dividends. Here are some examples of such files:

- Letterhead
- Memo Template
- Fax Cover
- Purchase Order Form
- Backup for Administrative Software
- Financial Spreadsheet
- Expense Form
- Meeting Planner

I handle these frequently-used files by creating a folder on the desktop called *Fingertip*. It contains those few files which receive constant use. Double-clicking on that one folder puts the collection *at my fingertips*.

Current Projects

The *Current Projects* folder is a place for all of the digital information related to a project in progress. My Current Projects file resides on the desktop. Every item in the Current Projects folder is linked to the task list. On the task list, I place a "(CP)" beside a task that has supporting material in the Current Projects folder.

When I complete a task or a project that had the "(CP)" beside it, whatever was in the Current Project file must go somewhere else. Digital project information is treated just like the paper project information material housed in the tickler files. When the project has been completed, a decision must be made about what project information to retain and what to delete. If the material is of lasting value, I *clean up* the digital material, getting rid of any individual documents not needed. I then drag the material into the digital reference system in My Documents.

Backing Up Your Files

"How many of you have a good system for backing up your files?" When this question is asked of a typical group of professionals, few if any hands are raised. When defining what is meant by a *good system* of backing up, it must be one that is *easy enough you will actually do it.*

Before discussing a backup system, one must realize basically two types of hard drives exist:

1. Those that have crashed

2. Those that will crash

These sobering thoughts should set the tone for wanting to learn and apply a good backup system.

To put the importance of this skill in perspective, examine what would happen if the hard drive crashed today. With one phone call, you could probably summon the help of someone with the technical skills to get the computer up and going again. The job would entail purchasing and installing a new hard drive. This part is relatively inexpensive. The operating system resides on a set of CD-ROMs that came with the computer. Your tech-savvy friend can reinstall those. The programs which were on the computer can be reloaded from CD-ROMs. You can now resume using your computer just as you had before.

Without a good backup system, what will be *lost forever*?

- The Student Handbook: Do you really want to be faced with having to rekey that entire document?

- Faculty Handbook: Rekeying that document will be a major time commitment.

- The entire packet related to that big field trip you sponsor every year: Gone are the introductory letter, release forms, itinerary, and lesson plans preparing the students for the trip and providing follow-up activities after the trip. All the well-crafted material you honed over the years is now history!

- Your term paper: You have been working on that paper for your graduate class every night for the last 3 weeks, not to mention spending all of last week on it. The paper is due the day after tomorrow. Imagine the feeling of panic at having to recreate the paper from scratch.

With so much importance resting with our data, why do so few people have a system for protecting it from disaster? For most the answer is easy. *Nobody ever showed them how.* Even if they tried to do a backup, what exactly needs to be copied? The computer has hundreds of thousands of files. Where would they even begin?

The answer is simple. During the discussion setting up a digital filing system and saving files throughout this chapter, where have we talked about saving them? The answer is exactly three places:

1. My Documents
2. Fingertip
3. Current Projects

Because you are only saving to those three places, you only have to back up those three files!

The following procedure provides a system that ensures your data is safe. In addition, it is easy enough *you will actually do it*:

- Insert a flash drive into a vacant USB port.

- Double click on My Computer. Your screen should look like Figure 8.6.

- Double-click on the picture of the flash drive. The contents of the flash drive are displayed. There may not be anything on it, or there may be some other files previously saved.

- Create a new folder inside the flash drive (Right-click > New > Folder). Name it with the current month and year. Double-click on that folder to open it.

- Double-click on My Documents. You are now looking at two windows. One (My Documents) contains all your files. The other (the folder on your flash drive) is the place where the files will be copied. Hold down the Control (Ctrl) key and simultaneously press the "A" key for *Select All*.

- All the documents are highlighted. Figure 8.7 provides an example of how these two folders may appear.

- Click on any one of those files and drag it into the window on your flash drive. All the rest of the documents will follow. As the files are copying, you see a box with pieces of paper flying across from one folder to another (Figure 8.8).

Figure 8.6. Inserting a Flash Drive for Backup

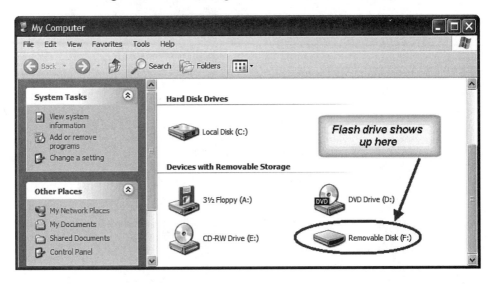

Figure 8.7. Folders Ready to Copy

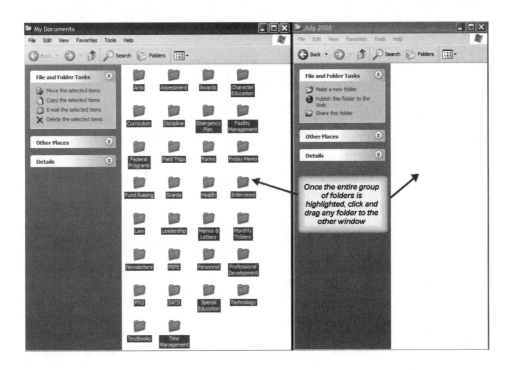

Figure 8.8. Files Being Copied

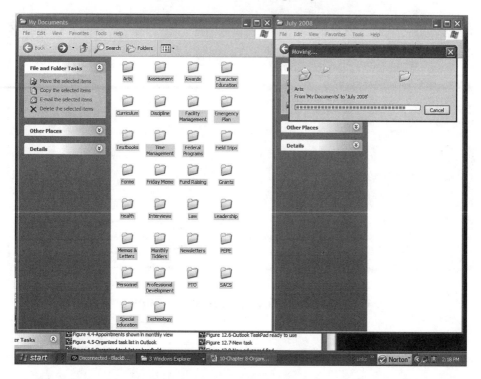

Provided your flash drive has enough storage space, simply sit back and relax while the files back up to the flash drive. If you do not have enough room on your flash drive, as many files as possible are copied, and a message pops up prompting the insertion of a second flash drive. At that point remove that flash drive and insert another. However, the best advice is to invest in a flash drive with more memory. The process must be easy, and having a flash drive that stores the entire job is a major part of making things easy. At this point, simply repeat the process with the Fingertip and Current Projects files. The process is complete.

How often should this backup routine occur? There is no one answer. I backup My Documents monthly and both Fingertip and Current Projects weekly. If I work on one document for an entire day or more, I back up that particular document at the end of the day.

A flash drive is the tool used in this chapter as the medium for backing up data. As this book goes to press, a flash drive is the best answer for most people. One could use a set of floppy disks; however, this process may easily require a dozen floppy disks. When backing up pictures, one large picture by itself could exceed the storage capacity of a floppy disk.

One CD-ROM may be able to hold all your data, unless many pictures must be copied. If the amount of data is large, an external hard drive is a good investment. With a large-capacity flash drive or an external hard drive, many months of backups may be stored. Each backup simply is in its own folder and labeled with the name of the month and year.

Once you become comfortable with this process, it will become intuitive. Open a window for where your data is now. Open a window for where the data needs to go. *Select All* and drag. It does not get any easier than that!

As this chapter concludes, these points are true about your computer:

◆ You can file easily and logically.

◆ You can find files later.

◆ You are not going to lose all your files if the hard drive crashes!

Now you have a system you can trust!

Next Steps

◆ Examine your paper reference filing system for any needing reorganization.

◆ List the digital files you need for your digital reference files.

◆ Create all of the needed files in My Documents.

◆ Drag all the documents currently on your computer to their proper folders within My Documents.

◆ Create your Fingertip and Current Projects files on the desktop. Drag to those files any documents that belong there.

◆ Decide what to use to backup your files, and secure whatever you need.

◆ Include an entry on your Repeating Task List each month to remind you to backup your files.

◆ Include an entry on your Repeating Task List each month to remind you to check the Monthly Tickler.

9

E-Mail and Other Electronic Timesavers

Home is where you hang your @.

Author Unknown

E-Mail: Time Management Tool or Time Sink?

Is e-mail a great time-management tool or a great time sink? In little more than a decade, it moved from being a rare novelty to being commonplace. We all love it, because it is easy to send a message to one person or to hundreds of people with a single mouse click. We hate it because our e-mail Inbox explodes with advertisements, jokes, and a host of other low-priority items. We stress about it because we also get good information and do not know exactly what to do with it.

E-mail is the most efficient means of communication available in the world of education. Even if phones existed in all classrooms, statistics from the business world show that approximately 20% of calls are completed the first time. With e-mail, messages are sent at a time convenient for the sender. They are read at a time convenient for the recipient. *Telephone tag* is gone forever.

In addition, e-mail allows the other party to do the necessary research before replying. We have all been caught off-guard by a telephone call where the caller asked for information we did not have available. E-mail eliminates the awkward game of "I'll get that information and get back with you."

Decision, Decisions:
Getting from *In* to *Empty*

Imagine for a moment a person has just arrived home from work. He walks to the curb and takes the mail from the mailbox. He opens the mail and reads it. He then walks back to the curb and puts all the mail back in the mailbox. The next day, when he walks to the mailbox, he finds today's mail sitting on top of yesterday's mail. After several more days, he needs to buy a bigger mailbox! Even worse, the person hates that walk to the curb because he knows what mess awaits him.

This scenario sounds crazy, doesn't it? Yet it is exactly how all too many people approach their e-mail Inboxes. They read it, and because they don't know exactly what to do with it, they leave it. It is not uncommon to see an Inbox that contains every piece of e-mail the owner has received since the computer came out of the box! We would not stand for this situation with the mailbox by the curb. Why do we allow it for its digital counterpart?

When you walk away from your mailbox, it is empty. Better yet, it's not empty just one day. It is empty at the end of every day. How great it would be if only the e-mail Inbox operated like the mailbox by the curb?

The key to getting an empty Inbox is to make simple decisions about each and every item. Therefore, make a practice of only looking at your e-mail when you have the time and energy to make those decisions. At that point, go from top to bottom and make small decisions at each turn.

Delete It

Much e-mail requires no action other than to briefly scan it and hit the delete key. Examples include advertisements of no interest, jokes, threads from e-mail discussion groups, and for-your-information courtesy copies. Many people find it helpful to sort the e-mail by *conversation.* All mail related to a single subject then appears together. If the subject is of no interest, delete the entire thread at one time.

Do It

Some e-mails require only a quick response. Give that response immediately and then delete the mail if it is of no further value. What if the response is going to take some time and possibly some research? In that case send a quick response to let the person know the message has been received and you will be getting back with them. Using Microsoft Outlook, drag the e-mail to the Task icon, assign a due date, and change the subject line as needed. Now delete the e-mail.

Forward It

Perhaps someone else really needs to handle this message. Simply forward the message to the appropriate person and delete the e-mail. If you should happen to need it later, go to Sent Items and view what had been forwarded.

Save It

What if the information may be of lasting value? This type of e-mail message poses more trouble than any other. We know the information may be needed again but simply do not know what to do with it. Let's break the scenario down a little further and look at specific suggestions:

- *The text of the e-mail is of lasting value for documentation purposes.* The reason for saving this information is so that it can be retrieved should someone ask for it. The value lies in lending proof of what was communicated and when. If you use Microsoft Outlook to organize, drag the e-mail over the Notes icon. Edit the note as needed and save. The note is automatically date and time stamped upon creation. A second option is to save the e-mail in Memos & Letters in My Documents. To do this, go to the e-mail program's File menu and choose Save As. Navigate to the Memos & Letters folder and save.

- *The text of the e-mail is of lasting value because of the subject matter.* For example, the text of the message contains a good set of questions for teacher interviews. Rather than save this message in the Memos & Letters folder, I would save it in the Personnel Management folder, which is also located in My Documents. If inside the Personnel Management folder an Interview Questions folder existed, that subfolder would be the ideal place. Before saving, I would edit the name of the e-mail to best reflect the contents.

- *The e-mail has an attachment of lasting value for documentation.* Drag the attachment to the Memos & Letters file. Rename the document with the name of the sender followed by a dash and a few words descriptive of the subject.

- *The e-mail has an attachment of lasting value because of the subject matter.* Drag the attachment to the proper folder inside My Documents. If the attachment consisted of a set of teacher interview questions, I would it drag to the Personnel Management folder inside My Documents.

In Becomes Empty

The important point is that a decision is made about each piece of e-mail the first time the message is read. Junk is deleted. Items requiring action receive action and are then deleted. Items for someone else's attention are forwarded to them, and then deleted. Material to save is saved as a note in Microsoft Outlook, saved in Memos & Letters, or saved at some other appropriate place in My Documents. The message is then deleted. Soon, *In* becomes *Empty*.

Delegating by E-Mail

Often, the purpose of an e-mail message is to ask someone else to do something. The ball is in the other person's court, but we still have the obligation to follow up and ensure the other person delivers.

A simple technique for follow-up is to send yourself a copy of the message. In addition to the *To* and *CC* (carbon copy) lines, every e-mail program has a line called BCC, which stands for *blind courtesy (or carbon) copy*. The difference between CC and BCC is significant. When an address is placed in the CC line, all other recipients can see that this person received a copy. When an address in placed in the BCC line, the person receives copy of the message, but no other recipient will know it. When delegating a task to someone else via e-mail, simply put yourself in the BCC line. The next time you check your e-mail, a copy of that message arrives in the Inbox and serves as a reminder to follow up.

What do you do with that reminder? Drag the e-mail over the task icon, which automatically creates a new task in Microsoft Outlook with all the appropriate information completed. Assign a due date, assign a status of "Waiting for someone else," and save. The e-mail message can be deleted. A reminder to follow up now resides on the task list.

Sent Items:
Your Permanent Record

One reason I prefer e-mail over other forms of communication is that it provides an instant record of what we told other people and when we told them. By clicking Sent Items and typing a keyword into the search box, you can put your hands on practically any message you have sent. The list can also be sorted by date or recipient, allowing needed information to be found quickly.

Should there be any disagreement over what had been discussed via e-mail, referring to the Sent Items and forwarding to the other person a copy of the pertinent e-mail message clears up all doubt.

Minimizing Spam

Spam probably tops the list of things we hate about e-mail. Microsoft Outlook is equipped with an excellent *spam filter*. The filter identifies what it considers spam and presents it in a list of *Junk E-mail*. One can actually teach the filter to become more accurate. If the filter allows a message through from a sender whose mail you do not wish to receive, simply right-click on the message and choose *Add to Blocked Senders List*. By the same token, if legitimate e-mail shows up in the junk mail, right-click on the message and select *Add to Safe Senders List*.

Under no circumstances should anyone reply to spam by asking to be removed from the list. Replying to spam tells the spammers that they have hit on a real e-mail address. Not only that, but the spammers know they have found someone who is not only diligent about reading e-mail, but someone who responds to the e-mail received. Replying to spam makes you a spammer's dream! Stand back and watch the Inbox overflow with spam! A better solution is to use the delete key and give the spammers not another thought. You have better ways to spend your time than to fume about spammers.

Be Part of the Solution by Not Being Part of the Problem

E-mail is the medium of choice for such time-wasting activities as forwarding jokes and hoaxes. Because sending to your entire address book is as easy as sending to a single individual, cyberspace is flooded with junk. I have made a personal decision to use the delete key. Although some of the jokes are funny and provide a good chuckle, forwarding them to a large group is something I choose not to do.

Run for Your Life! It's a Hoax!

Hoaxes are a bit different from other junk e-mail in that the people who forward them think they are being helpful. The hoaxes typically promise free merchandise when forwarded to a certain number of people or provide warnings about which everyone must be informed. As school leaders we can educate those around us about how to expose a hoax before innocently forwarding it.

Revealing a hoax for what it is takes all of 5 seconds and is remarkably simple to do. You can easily show your staff how to perform the following test on any suspected hoax:

♦ Highlight a couple of sentences of text from the e-mail and use the Copy command (Control [Ctrl]+C).

♦ Open your Internet browser and navigate to Google (http://www.google.com) or any other reliable search engine.

♦ Click in the search line and use the paste command (Ctrl+V).

♦ Press *Enter*.

♦ The search results tell you instantly whether or not you have hooked a hoax. If the message is a hoax, the titles on the search results received make it obvious.

Some people look at hoaxes as harmless fun. Wasting work time, contributing to the problem of junk e-mail in everyone's Inbox, and clogging up your employer's server is anything but *simple, harmless fun*. Other hoaxes are actually more harmful. Take, for example, the Teddy Bear Hoax. Readers were warned about a virus and told how to search for a particular file. If the file was present, the computer was infected. The e-mail would go on to explain how to get rid of the infected file. Finally, the e-mail would ask that people forward the e-mail to everyone else. It seemed everyone receiving the e-mail was finding that indeed, they did have this suspect file on their computers. In actuality, a good reason existed for everyone seeming to have this suspect file. Everyone was supposed to have that file! It is a part of Microsoft Windows and serves a good function! Of course, the problem each of them faced then was figuring out how to get the deleted file back again.

Whenever you get one of these suspect e-mails, try this drill:

♦ Under no circumstances add to the problem by forwarding the hoax.

♦ Use the copy-Google-paste routine described earlier.

♦ Copy the URL of one of the sites that explains the hoax.

♦ Go back to the e-mail and hit Reply.

♦ Paste the URL into the message.

♦ Just above the link and before hitting Send, I generally include the message, "Run for your life! It's a hoax!"

Gaining Newspaper Coverage

Do you feel your local paper is consistently there to cover the good things that happen in your school? School leaders are usually quick to lament the lack of coverage of the positive and the emphasis on the negative. My experience has been the newspapers are usually glad to print what is given them, provided it is delivered to the right person and the job is made easy for them. E-mail is the answer.

Telephone the paper and ask for the name and e-mail address of the person to whom school-related material should be sent. When newsworthy events happen, e-mail the story to the appropriate person. This process eliminates the need to drive to the paper and search for the person who should receive this type of the material. The newspaper reporter is relieved of the job of rekeying the copy into his computer. From his perspective, the job is a simple copy and paste from your e-mail to his computer. You have just made covering the good news happening in your school *easy enough the newspaper will include it*! Your story, along with the digital photo you include as an attachment, will most likely find its way into the paper.

Other E-Mail Tricks

- ◆ Check e-mail only at designated points in the day. E-mail becomes an interruption and a time-waster when we check it constantly throughout the day.

- ◆ Handle all e-mail in one group. Go from the top of the list and do not stop until you reach the bottom. Make a decision about each e-mail. Act on the e-mails that require action, or at least add items to your task list describing what needs to be done. Respond to those that simply need a response. Forward what needs to be forwarded. File what needs to be filed. Delete what needs to be deleted. When you get to the bottom of the list, the Inbox should be empty.

- ◆ Delay checking e-mail until midmorning. Begin the day with the tasks you *planned* to begin your day. Once the day is shaping up as planned, you are likely to handle e-mail quickly and get back to working through your task list. If you begin the day with e-mail, you may well get so wrapped up in reading and responding that the day gets away with little actually being accomplished.

- ◆ Create subject lines that are descriptive of the message. The person who receives your e-mail can tell a great deal about the contents without even opening it. Although a subject line reading, "Meeting," conveys little, a subject line reading, "Staff meeting October 23 at 9:00 in the Board Room," gives the receiver a much clearer picture of the nature and importance of the message. At times, the entire message can be put in the subject line. "Your leave request was approved," "The figures you needed are attached," and "Can you meet with me Friday at 2:00?" are examples of how one can convey the entire message in the subject line.

◆ Keep messages short. If at all possible, limit the message to one screen of text. If the message runs longer, look to see if perhaps several different subjects are being covered in the same message. If so, consider breaking the e-mail into several short messages, each handling a different subject.

◆ Front-load the message. Begin by giving the reader an idea of what to *do* about your message. Include the most important information toward the beginning of the message. Let the less important details bring up the tail end.

◆ Save time by creating a signature line. The signature line can include anything you like. Typically, your name, title, organization, address, telephone, fax, and e-mail address are good information to include. The signature line is to the e-mail what letterhead is to written correspondence. Consulting the *Help* feature of any e-mail program provides instruction on how to create a signature in that program.

◆ Avoid printing e-mail messages. The advantage of digital data is the ease with which it can be stored, searched, retrieved, shared, or edited. Printing digital data negates all these advantages. People often print e-mail because they are simply used to handling paper. Old habits can be hard to break.

Using Administrative Software to the Fullest

As recent as a generation ago, schools managed administrative tasks by dividing them among the faculty and letting everyone share the load. Today, the school administrative package loaded on office computers has the capability to produce honor roll lists, average end-of-year grades, address envelopes, and conduct countless clerical tasks that were so time-consuming not so many years ago.

Many of today's school leaders remember performing these clerical tasks during their early years in the teaching field. Unfortunately, many continue to farm out these clerical tasks to already overwhelmed teachers without stopping to consider how their administrative software could accomplish the same tasks more accurately in a fraction of the time.

Many other school leaders, however, make their administrative software sing like a well-tuned violin. The difference between those who harness the power of this technology and those who do not seems to lie with the habit of asking one simple question. Before asking teachers to assimilate data or perform any of these other clerical functions, the savvy school leader asks the question, "Can I get the computer to do this for me?" The answer was usually yes. Asking the questions puts one half way toward finding the answer.

The school leader who wants to improve in the ability to use school administrative software will benefit from these suggestions:

- If you find yourself handwriting student data, *stop*! Ask if the information can be produced by the software, and do not necessarily take no for an answer. When people say, "It can't be done," they so often mean, "I don't know how to do it."

- Read the manual *cover to cover*. You will be surprised at the capabilities you would have never thought were present. Not only does the manual answer the questions, it reveals answers to questions you did not know to ask.

- Use telephone technical support. The school probably pays an annual fee for technical support, so get your money's worth. Keep the telephone number handy. When a question arises, telephone the people whose business it is to know that piece of software forward and backward.

One example of holding on to practices of the past when a much more efficient practice exists today is in the area of collecting student demographic data at the beginning of the school year. The universally accepted method before 1990 or so was to send a home a form printed on a large index card for parents to complete. That card was then filed in the main office. Perhaps the school sent home several such cards. One was filed in the office, another in the counselor's office, and a third might be kept by the homeroom teacher. If an address, telephone numbers, or names of persons allowed to check the child out from school had changed from the previous year, filling out new cards at the beginning of the year ensured accurate data.

Today when we need an address or telephone number, we look up the data on our computers rather than consult cards. However, many schools continue the same practice of sending home the annual index card as a means of keeping their data current. Using this procedure, the only way to be sure the information in the computer is accurate would be to examine each piece of data on the card versus each piece of data on the computer. The task would be unreasonably labor intensive.

The solution to the problem is so simple. Prior to the opening day of school, the administrative assistant prints from the computer a demographic sheet for each student. Most school software packages have such a report already formatted. The parent is then asked to examine the sheet and prominently mark anything that has changed. The administrative assistant then simply flips through the forms looking for items parents have marked and makes corrections on the computer during the process. Once all corrections have been made, the demographic forms are retained for those emergencies, such as when the electricity may go out.

Search the Internet

My generation grew up in a time when finding information was a time-consuming task. All but the most elementary research included getting in the car and driving to a large library, combing the card catalog, consulting the *Reader's Guide to Periodical Literature,* and then going on a safari through row after row of books to physically lay hands on one book after another.

Research has become much easier, to say the least. One 30-second online search garners more information than a week in the library. The improvement opportunity for many school leaders is to make an Internet search our first thought. Yes, we may be able to uncover the same information by scouring books and periodicals in our offices. An Internet search often puts the same or similar information at our fingertips in seconds.

Searching the Internet for information is an exceptional time-saver when we need to have information in digital format. Suppose one is preparing a newsletter and wishes to include a certain lengthy poem. Having the poem at hand, many school leaders would have the administrative assistant key the lengthy poem into the computer. The tech-savvy school leader would let an Internet search find the poem. A single copy and paste puts the poem into the newsletter in seconds.

School leaders save time when they ask if the school administrative software can give them needed data rather than ask a team of teachers to collect it. By the same token, school leaders save time for themselves and those around them when they first consider the search capabilities of the Internet before using less efficient means of collecting data.

The School Leader's Blog

Short for *weblog*, a *blog* is a quick and easy way for the school leader to have a presence on the Internet and communicate with an audience. A teacher's blog may communicate with students in the class as well as the parents. A principal's blog may be used to communicate with staff or parents. At the central office level, a blog might be designed to communicate with the staff at each school or the community as a whole.

My own experience with blogging began as a follow-up to my workshops. The blog served as a means to maintain contact with workshop participants long after the workshop had concluded. During my final year as a principal, I created two blogs. One was designed to communicate with the staff, and replaced the paper memo I used religiously since coming to that school. Each week, a new blog post provided information the staff needed during the week. A second blog was used as a vehicle to communicate with parents. In this case the blog replaced the paper newsletters I was producing.

When I moved from the principalship to the central office, creating two blogs was one of the first orders of business. One was designed to provide news and information from our schools and central office to the community. The second was created to serve as a tool to communicate with all our employees. Designated people at each school could compose posts to these blogs. In this way news from every school is organized in one place.

Every week information comes across my desk that needs to be passed on the teachers at all schools. If it were not for the staff blog, communicating that information would consist of a trip to the copier to produce copies for each school. Principals at each school would then be asked to communicate the information to their teachers. Usually, this process would involve reproducing copies at their schools and stuffing those in teacher mailboxes.

With the staff blog, as information comes across the desk, I compose a quick post and include a link where teachers can find all the necessary information. In less than 5 minutes, the process is complete.

A blog offers the following advantages:

◆ Blogs are easy to compose.

◆ The price is right. Many sites allow the user to establish a blog for free. No special software is required. An Internet connection is all that is needed.

◆ Blogs are easy to maintain. New posts appear at the top of the blog. Each post is automatically date and time stamped.

◆ You have an automatic history of everything you have posted. All previous posts are maintained in chronological order from the most recent to the most ancient.

- You can post pictures. Any digital photograph or piece of digital clipart that can be downloaded to the computer desktop can be posted on your blog.
- You can insert links in any post. With one click, teachers or community members can be directed to any spot on the Internet you wish them to visit.

Next Steps

- Empty your e-mail Inbox using the method described in this chapter.
- Decide on your method for following up on items delegated by e-mail. A BCC to yourself will do the job.
- Sort your e-mail Inbox by conversation. Right-click on the title bar and make your selection.
- Call your local newspaper to get the name and e-mail address of the proper person for school news. Put this contact information in your e-mail program.
- Find the telephone number for your administrative software technical support. Put this number in your signature tool.
- Locate the instruction manual for your school administrative software. Add reading that manual to your task list. Suggest that others who use the software on a regular basis do the same.
- Examine the data you ask other people to gather. Determine how much information can be pulled from your administrative software.
- Determine if you would like to start a blog of your own.

10

Focused or Fragmented?

The enemy often tries to make us attempt and start many projects so that we will be overwhelmed with too many tasks, and therefore achieve nothing and leave everything unfinished. Sometimes he even suggests the wish to undertake some excellent work that he foresees we will never accomplish. This is to distract us from the prosecution of some less excellent work that we would have easily completed. He does not care how many plans and beginnings we make, provided nothing is finished.

St. Francis de Sales

School leaders face the dilemma of limited time versus a seemingly unlimited number of projects. Furthermore, we would like to devote our attention to anyone who needs it at any given moment. Our days become fragmented. We leave in the evening feeling nothing has been accomplished and that we are further behind today than yesterday. That feeling may be what prompted you to read this book. The quote beginning this chapter is a cautionary tale to us all.

To this point the book has provided a system to organize papers, appointments, tasks, repeating tasks, documentation, and the computer. In short, the tools are in place to organize all the obligations you have accepted. This chapter explores our ability to choose. We have the ability to say "No," "Not now," and "Not me" far more than we choose to.

Work From an Organized List

The old adage, "Plan your work and work your plan," is good advice for a busy school leader. Handling challenges as they are thrown at us does keep us busy; however, it is an inefficient and ineffective way to work. You have learned how to construct an organized task list, which groups similar items together. Furthermore, you have learned how to make the list crystal clear. When looking at a task, you know exactly how to accomplish it. The list has a natural *flow*.

The strategy we must develop in a world filled with interruptions is to work our list. Instead of allowing e-mail, cell phones, and drop-in visitors to derail our train of thought, we can use e-mail, voice mail, and human *gatekeepers* to trap incoming data. Later in the day, we look at all the new inputs as a group and plan how to respond. Although the ringing and dinging of our digital interrupters gives the impression of urgency, the truth is that virtually all of them can wait.

Work from the list, and you ensure you are getting the most done in a given amount of time. You eliminate hopping back and forth between tasks. Few people realize how much time and energy is required to refocus on the work at hand once it is interrupted. The more you jump from project to project, the more time you waste.

Quiet Hour

Statistics show that the average executive is interrupted anywhere from every 8 minutes to every 3 minutes. Refocusing after an interruption may take 15 minutes. With statistics such as these, is it any wonder we leave work feeling we have accomplished nothing?

Imagine two people of similar ability. You know that you can call Person A at any time. E-mail him and receive a response within a few minutes every time. Drop in anytime and find an *open door*. To this point the scenario sounds appealing. Realize, however, that when Person A is working on a project for *you*, this person stops to answer every phone call, respond to every e-mail, and see anyone who wishes to stop by for a chat. The project you thought would be completed in several days drags on for weeks.

Person B is harder to access *immediately*. A well-trained secretary protects this person's time from drop-in visitors. Person B returns your calls and e-mails within the day, but not within minutes. Yet, when working on a project for *you*, Person B is focused on that project and that project alone. The project is completed accurately and in a timely fashion.

Which person would you rather have working with you? Furthermore, which person's time would you respect more?

To accomplish anything of substance, you must establish some uninterrupted time during the day, often called the *Quiet Hour.* For the school leader who is in the classroom, one's planning period would likely serve as that time. For building-level administrators, this time might occur shortly after the beginning of the school day after all students are in class and before problems in classrooms arise. Whether this amount of time is actually 1 hour, 2 hours, or half an hour is not important. What is important is that time is blocked out daily. The other important point is that a plan exists for how that time will be used.

School leaders most likely need the assistance of a *gatekeeper* to help protect their time. In most situations, the administrative assistant who answers the telephone and greets visitors serves in this role. If this person puts through every phone call and drop-in visitor, your time is not your own. My experience has been that simply letting the gatekeeper know how you want these situations handled is enough. We all have a few individuals whose calls we want to be put through to us. For other callers the gatekeeper can determine the nature of the call. You can gather needed information before returning the call, thus saving time for both you and the caller.

For the building-level administrator, one excellent technique for avoiding interruptions during the day is to be accessible in the morning before the start of classes. Walking the halls as students and teachers arrive provides an opportunity for a brief encounter with any teacher who needs one. If they know they have this daily opportunity, they are less likely to appear at the office door while you are trying to concentrate on a project.

You Teach Other People How to Treat You

When working on an important project and someone drops in, what do you do? If you drop the project and let this person have as much of your time as desired, get ready for a repeat performance. Do you respond to every e-mail as soon as it rolls in? If so, others come to expect it and are upset if they do not receive an instant response. Basically, you teach those around you how to treat you by what you allow. Furthermore, you teach others how you value your own time by how well or poorly you manage it.

When someone waits until the 11th hour to drop a task in your lap, how do you handle the situation? If you bail the other person out, the lesson you teach is that others can wait until the last minute and you will still make sure everything turns out just fine. Prepare for more of the same.

Do you find yourself unable to tackle valuable tasks because you are answering insignificant questions posed in e-mail and handling other trite requests? If you continue to work through your organized task list and handle these interrupters last rather than first, interesting things begin to happen. People try and find answers on their own before turning their research projects over to you. When they see that you have a plan for your time, they find someone else to handle the trivial tasks.

Another side to this scenario exists. As you assume projects of significance and produce results, a clear message is sent that you are the person for this type of assignment. Do you wish to spend your time on the trivial or the significant? Ultimately, that choice is yours. You teach people how to treat you.

How Much Can You Do Well?

We are capable of handling a great number of projects. We simply cannot work on all of them simultaneously. A large part of maintaining your sanity has to do with learning to say, "Not now." The signature tool is your friend when it comes to trapping those projects that you cannot accept now but want to accomplish in the future.

If you organize with paper, Chapter 3 discusses using a Future Tasks page in the back of the planner to record worthy tasks, projects, or goals that you cannot begin now. For those who organize digitally, add these items to the TaskPad and assign a date sometime in the future to consider them again. In either case, you can now concentrate on the task at hand. All other worthwhile projects wait their turn.

Who Can Help? The Art of Delegation

Elementary school teachers are masters of delegation. One student is in charge of changing the calendar date. Someone else passes out papers. A third student is in charge of feeding the classroom hamster. The list goes on and on.

Elementary school teachers understand something so many of us miss. None of us can do everything. Others can do some of those things as well as we can. Sharing the load not only frees us to do tasks that only we can do, it gives others a stake in the program. Look for the repeating tasks. The routine things that must be done each day, week, or month are prime candidates for delegation. As others assume some of these tasks, your time becomes free for those things only you can do.

What Really Does Not Need to Be Done?

How many reports does your organization generate simply because *that is the way we have always done it*? Doing well that which need not be done at all is a terrible waste of time. If you are trying to find time for worthwhile projects, getting rid of the unnecessary is a great place to start.

Next Steps

- Identify the time, or times, of day you want to establish as Quiet Hours.
- Plan how you to approach your gatekeeper and what instructions to give.
- Decide what times of the day are best to check and handle voice mail and e-mail.
- Examine your task list to determine what items you could delegate and to whom you could delegate them.
- Examine your task list to determine what items need not be done at all, and get rid of them.

11

Conclusion: Time is Your Friend

Dost thou love life? Then do not squander time, for that's the stuff life is made of.

Benjamin Franklin

This book began with a poem I stumbled on quite a few years ago in a work called *The Harried Leisure Class* (Linder, 1970). On the page facing this poem is a simple quote by Dennis Gabor, "Till now man has been up against nature; from now on he will be up against his own nature." (Linder, 1970, p. x)

The nature of our society implores us to do more, increase complexity, and ignore the finiteness of the time available. Our schools reflect these same tendencies, and our school leaders find themselves facing enormous demands with limited time in which to address them.

You hardly need anyone to point out these realities. More than likely, these are the very concerns that lead you to this book. My hope is that this book has provided an understandable framework. Our jobs are not the papers and e-mails that come at us from all sides. The inability to handle them, however, hampers our ability to be school leaders. Each chapter is crafted to give you the *nuts and bolts* of structuring a system equal to the demands of the job.

Every reader is different, and for this reason some strategies resonate more with you than others. A colleague may read the same book and take from it entirely different ideas for organizing life and managing time. I hope that this book earns a place close at hand, complete with highlighted sentences, margins filled with notes, and pages dog-eared to mark their easy retrieval. Each reading is likely to reveal a previously unrealized nuance.

In the introductory chapter, we defined the *school leader* as someone who steps forward to help shape the direction of what happens in schools, regardless of the title on the job description. As this book comes to a close, I hope you found strategies to make your job easier, your stress level lower, and confidence in your ability to assume a strong leadership role at an all-time high. The school leader needs the tools that make the complex simple, and this book has aimed to provide them.

Every good thing we do for our students, our school systems, our communities, our families, and ourselves is accomplished through the dimension of time. For the organized school leader, time is a friend.

Appendix

Configuring
Microsoft Outlook

Getting Acquainted With Microsoft Outlook

When opening Microsoft Outlook for the first time, you may receive a message asking if you want Microsoft Outlook to be your default e-mail program. For now answer no to that question. If you decide for sure that Microsoft Outlook is the program for you, do not worry. Microsoft Outlook will ask this question the next time and each time the program is opened until you finally answer yes.

Microsoft Outlook's prompts will guide the process of establishing an e-mail account. You need to know what type of server used to retrieve your e-mail (Microsoft Exchange Server, Pop3, IMP, HTTP, or other type of server). Secure this information from your service provider if you do not already know it. You also need to know your e-mail address and password associated with your account.

These seven steps allow the most efficient use of Microsoft Outlook:

1. On the left-hand side of the screen, notice the series of buttons similar to those shown in Figure App.1. This area is called the *navigation pane*. Click the Calendar button

2. From the menu bar at the top of the screen, choose View > Arrange By > Show Views in Navigation Pane. A series of radio buttons appear in the navigation pane.

3. Click the "Day/Week/Month" radio button (Figure App.2).

4. We want to show the TaskPad if it is not already showing. From the menu bar, select View > TaskPad.

5. Select View > TaskPadView > Active Tasks for Selected Days.

6. Finally, return to View > TaskPad View. If "Include Tasks With No Due Date" does not have a check mark beside it, click on that selection.

7. The finished product should resemble Figure App.3.

Figure App.1. Selections in the Microsoft Outlook Navigation Pane

Figure App.2. Day/Week/Month View

Figure App.3. Outlook Day/Week/Month View With TaskPad

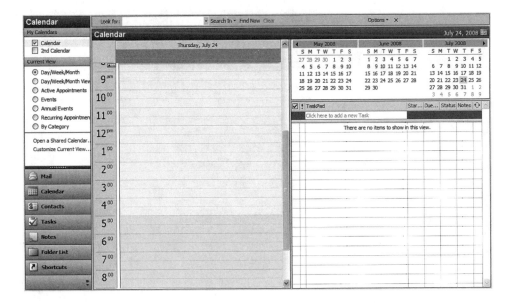

The Microsoft Outlook Calendar

Creating and working with appointments is intuitive. To create a new appointment, simply click on the calendar and type the name for an appointment. Click the mouse somewhere else, Microsoft Outlook accepts that appointment. For many appointments you schedule, what we have just done is sufficient.

To change the start and end times of an appointment, click the line at the top or bottom of the appointment and drag it to another time. Click in the middle of the appointment, and the entire appointment can be dragged to another time slot.

Double-clicking on an appointment opens a dialog box and reveals a number of variables you can control (Figure App.4).

Figure App.4. New Appointment

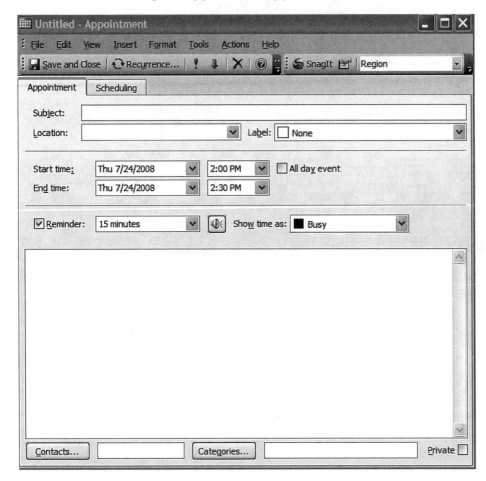

In this box, you have the ability to do the following:

◆ Choose a starting and ending date for the appointment.

◆ Choose a starting and ending time.

◆ Click Recurrence for an appointment that happens, for example, every Tuesday at 10:00 AM.

◆ Set a reminder. A box pops up and a chime sounds at the pre-scribed amount of time before the appointment.

◆ Enter notes related to the appointment. The large rectangular box provides a wealth of space to enter any details about that appointment.

All-Day Event

In addition to Appointments, which happen on a particular day at a particular time, you need to know how to create an *All Day Event*. The difference between the two is that the All-Day Event is not tied to a particular time. To create an All-Day Event, right-click directly on the date at the top of the calendar. Choose New All Day Event.

The TaskPad

Entering a new task could not be easier. When a new commitment presents itself, click where you see the message, "Click here to add a new Task," and press Enter. The task now appears on the list. Tasks not completed today will simply be there tomorrow. Even better, the TaskPad takes the responsibility for doing your remembering.

The first step is to set up the TaskPad:

- ◆ Right-click on the TaskPad header.
- ◆ A menu appears; select Customize Current View from that menu.
- ◆ A dialog box appears.
- ◆ Click on Fields. You may now select the fields to appear on the TaskPad.
- ◆ Where you see "Select available fields from," choose "Frequently-used fields."
- ◆ On the left-hand side of the box, click on each of the following fields in order, and click Add between each one. The fields you need are as follows:
  - Complete
  - Subject
  - Start Date
  - Due Date
  - Status (select Status if using a BlackBerry; select Category here if using a Palm)
  - Notes
  - Recurring

Figure App.5 shows how the dialog box looks. Before leaving this dialog box, do the following:

- ◆ Click the Filter button.
- ◆ Click the Advanced tab.

- From the Field menu, select Frequently-Used Fields > Complete.
- The Condition box should be set to "equals."
- Value should be No.
- Click Add to List.
- Click OK.
- Click OK.

Figure App.6 shows the finished product.

Figure App.5. Dialog Box Showing Microsoft Outlook Fields

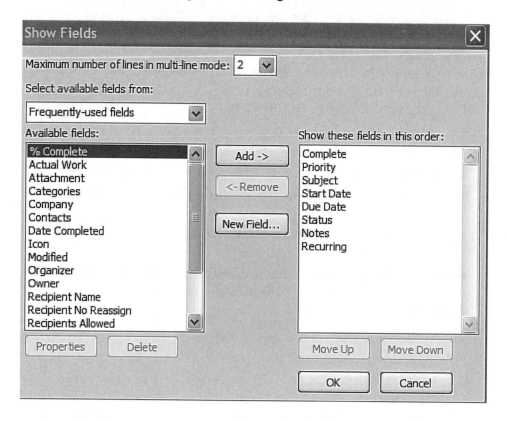

Figure App.6. Microsoft Outlook TaskPad Ready to Use

☑	!	TaskPad	Start Date	Due Date	Status	Notes	⟳
		Click here to add a new Task					
		There are no items to show in this view.					

Entering Sample Tasks

At this point, try entering a few sample tasks into the TaskPad. Click on the "Click here to add a Task" line, enter a sample task, and press Enter. The task appears in the list. Experiment with setting a start date or due date by clicking in the appropriate column and choosing a date from the pop-up calendar. Notice that by pressing Tab, you move across from field to field.

Headers in the TaskPad

The list can be sorted by clicking on any of the headers. Clicking the Due Date header sorts the list so that tasks overdue appear at the top and tasks due far in the future are at the bottom. Clicking on TaskPad sorts the list alphabetically by the name of the task. By clicking the Status header, you can see all the Not Started tasks together and all the tasks where you are Waiting on Someone Else together. To add a secondary sort, hold down the Shift key and click on a header.

Double-clicking a task displays the following elements over which the user has control. Figure App.7 shows the Task box.

- The name of the task goes in the Subject line.

- A date can be set for the task to appear on the list and to come due.

- A repeating pattern for the task can be established, such a reminder to change the air filters at home the 1st day of every month or order laminating film for the school every July 10th.

- Notes related to the task can be recorded in a large section. If the task is a phone call, take notes in that section during the call. If working on a project, list the first step in the subject line, and list the rest of known steps in the large note section. When one step is complete, instead of checking it off as done, cut and paste the next step into the subject line. Chapter 6, Handling Multiple Projects, discusses this concept in detail.

Figure App.7. New Task

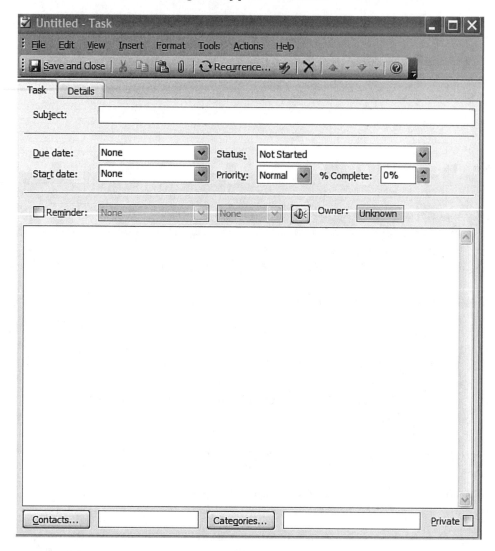

Keyboard Shortcuts

Microsoft Outlook allows the user to perform common commands with keyboard shortcuts. The shortcuts are much quicker than using the mouse to select those commands from menus. The shortcuts worth memorizing are:

Figure App.8. Keyboard Shortcuts

Keyboard Shortcut	Action Performed by Shortcut
Ctrl+Shift+A	Creates a new Appointment from anywhere in Microsoft Outlook
Ctrl+Shift+C	Creates a new Contact from anywhere in Microsoft Outlook
Ctrl+Shift+F	Creates an Advanced Find from anywhere in Microsoft Outlook
Ctrl+Shift+K	Creates a new Task from anywhere in Microsoft Outlook
Ctrl+Shift+M	Creates a new E-mail Message from anywhere in Microsoft Outlook
Ctrl+Shift+N	Creates a new Note from anywhere in Microsoft Outlook

Searching the TaskPad

You can search your Tasks at any time. Choosing Tools > Find > Advanced Find displays a search window as shown in Figure App.9. The keyboard shortcut Ctrl+Shift+F is much easier. Why would one need to search the task list?

- ◆ To satisfy yourself that you had indeed put a particular Task on the list, even if the start date was not to occur for months.
- ◆ To find a particular item you know was added to the list but somehow do not see it.
- ◆ To find a piece of information imbedded in the note section of a Task.
- ◆ To find a piece of information either in the subject line or note section of a Task completed sometime in the past.

Figure App.9. New Advanced Find

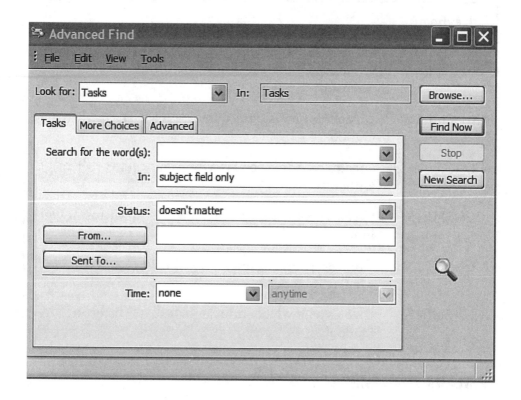

The default is to look for Appointments and Meetings. Change it to Tasks by selecting it from the pop-up menu. Microsoft Outlook will search "subject field only" or "subject and notes fields." Performing the "subject field only" search is much quicker and is the best choice if you are sure what is being sought is in the subject line. If searching for a piece of information possibly located in the notes, have Microsoft Outlook search "subject and notes fields."

Navigating the TaskPad

As you use the Microsoft Outlook TaskPad, assigning a Start Date and Due Date will be a skill set used numerous times every day. Likewise, you will change the Start Date and Due Date on various tasks. Microsoft Outlook offers shortcuts:

- ◆ You may select a Start Date and Due Date by clicking the arrow and navigating to a date using the calendar.

- You may type the date. For example, to enter the date January 20, 2009, you could enter any of the following:
  - 1/20/2009
  - 1/20/09
  - 1/20/9
- If the date you wish to select is within the current month, simply enter the day of the month. For example, entering "20" and pressing Tab enters the 20th day of the current month.
- If the date you wish to enter is within the next 12 months, you may enter the month and day. For example, entering "1/20" and pressing Tab assigns a date for the next January 20th.

In Chapter 4 we learned about organizing the TaskPad according to Due Date. We could then move tasks up or down the list by simply manipulating the Due Date. When entering a Due Date and pressing Enter, the cursor moves down to the Due Date field of the task below it. You can quickly alter the Due Date on a number of tasks by simply going down the list, entering the day of the month, and pressing Enter.

Maintaining Your Data

Backup Your *.pst* File

Your Microsoft Outlook data is valuable, and you certainly do not want to lose it because of a hard drive failure or problems with corruption. A critical concept to understand is that all your Microsoft Outlook data is located in one file. The extension of that file is going to be *.pst*. More than likely, the name of the file is going to be *Outlook.pst*.

To back up your Microsoft Outlook data, you need to know the location of that .pst file. To find it, go to File > Data File Management. Click on the Personal Folders line and then click Settings. In the new box, look at the File name line for the location of your Microsoft Outlook data. Figure App.10 illustrates what you will see.

Figure App.10. Location of .pst File

Close Microsoft Outlook before attempting to copy the Outlook.pst file. Otherwise, Microsoft Outlook returns an error message. Likewise, any other program that communicates with your Outlook.pst file may have to be closed also. For example, if you synchronize Microsoft Outlook to a handheld device, the program that manages your synchronization might need to be closed.

Now simply navigate to the Outlook.pst file. Right-click on it and choose Copy. Open My Documents and choose Paste. You now have a copy of your data in My Documents. The next time you make a backup of My Documents, a copy of your Microsoft Outlook data will be included in this backup. A free tool called "Microsoft Outlook Personal Folders Backup Tool," which simplifies the process, is available from Microsoft (http://office.microsoft.com).

Scanpst.exe

Scanpst.exe is a handy tool for diagnosing and repairing errors in the .pst file. Locating it can be tricky. I have found the easiest solution is to simply do a search for "scanpst." Once the search locates the file, right-click on it and create a shortcut. Drag the shortcut into your Fingertip file. Run this tool by double-clicking on it and following the simple instructions. Close Microsoft Outlook and any other program that may be accessing your Microsoft Outlook data before running the program; otherwise, an error message displays. Running scanpst.exe once a month serves as excellent preventive maintenance.

AutoArchive

AutoArchive removes older items from your .pst file and stores them in an archive file. The best course for the new Microsoft Outlook user is to simply turn off this feature. To perform this function, go to Tools > Options. Click Other Tab and then the AutoArchive button. Uncheck the box that says, "Run AutoArchive every ___ days." Figure App.11 shows how your screen should appear.

Figure App.11. AutoArchive Settings

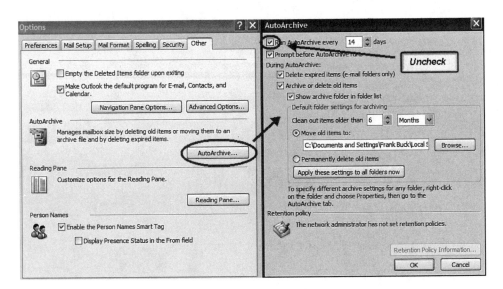

Once you have become experienced with Microsoft Outlook, you may wish to use AutoArchive. Simply return to the same screen shown in Figure App.11 and click the box to turn AutoArchive on. Select how often AutoArchive runs and how old items must be removed. The critical element here is that you do not allow your Notes to be AutoArchived. To prevent the Notes from being AutoArchived do the following (Figure App.12):

- ◆ Select Go > Folder List.
- ◆ Right-click on the Notes icon.
- ◆ Select Properties.
- ◆ Click the AutoArchive tab.
- ◆ Click the "Do not archive items in this folder" radio button.
- ◆ Click Apply and OK.

Figure App.12. Preventing AutoArchiving of Notes

Conclusion

Please refer back to this Appendix for the technical aspects involved with Microsoft Outlook. The instructions here allow you to get full benefit of the strategies in Chapter 4. As this book goes to press, Microsoft Outlook 2003 is the predominant version of the program. Microsoft Outlook 2007 has been released, and the similarity in the two versions makes the illustrations used here just as useable for the person using Microsoft Outlook 2007. Likewise, the coming years are sure to produce additional upgrades and a host of programs yet to be conceived.

The principles examined in this book are timeless, however. School leaders, both now and in the future, function in a complex world and require tools that make the complex simple. An understanding of the methodology in this book allows you to fashion any number of tools, both paper- and computer-based, into tools to help organize your life and manage your time.

References

Drucker, P. F. (1966). *The Effective Executive*. New York: Harper & Row.

Hobbs, C. R. (1987). *Time Power*. New York: Harper & Row.

Linder, S. B. (1970). *The Harried Leisure Class*. New York: Columbia University Press.

Mackenzie, R. A. (1972). *The Time Trap: How To Get More Done in Less Time*. New York: McGraw-Hill.

Mackenzie, Alec. (1990). *The Time Trap*. New York: AMACOM.

Pollar, Odette. (2007). *Get organized: What can it hurt? Day-Timer*. Retrieved 8 October, 2007 from www.daytimer.com/Time-Management-Resources/Get-Organized-What-Can-It-Hurt/0/False

Time/Design. Retrieved 8 October 2007 from www.timesystem.us